THE
AMERICAN COWBOY

Books by Harold McCracken, Litt.D.

IGLAOME (1930)

GOD'S FROZEN CHILDREN (1930)

PERSHING: THE STORY OF A GREAT SOLDIER (1931)

ALASKA BEAR TRAILS (1931)

BEYOND THE FROZEN FRONTIER (1936)

LAST OF THE SEA OTTERS (1942)

THE BIGGEST BEAR ON EARTH (1943)

SON OF THE WALRUS KING (1944)

SENTINEL OF THE SNOW PEAKS (1945)

THE GREAT WHITE BUFFALO (1946)

FREDERIC REMINGTON: ARTIST OF THE OLD WEST (1947)

TRAPPING: THE CRAFT OF CATCHING FUR-BEARING ANIMALS (1947)

TOUGHY: BULLDOG IN THE ARCTIC (1948)

CARIBOU TRAVELER (1949)

THE FLAMING BEAR (1951)

PORTRAIT OF THE OLD WEST (1952)

PIRATE OF THE NORTH (1953)

THE FREDERIC REMINGTON MEMORIAL COLLECTION (1954)

WINNING OF THE WEST (1955)

THE BEAST THAT WALKS LIKE MAN (1955)

THE STORY OF ALASKA (1956)

HUNTERS OF THE STORMY SEA (1957)

THE CHARLES M. RUSSELL BOOK (+ LTD. ED.) (1957)

HOOFS, CLAWS, AND ANTLERS (1958)

GOERGE CATLIN— AND THE OLD FRONTIER (+LTD. ED.) (1959)

FREDERIC REMINGTON'S OWN WEST (+LTD. ED.) (1960)

NICOLAI FECHIN (1961)

THE FREDERIC REMINGTON BOOK (+LTD. ED.) (1966)

ROUGHNECKS AND GENTLEMEN (1968)

"The Stampede"—W. R. LEIGH—Courtesy V. O. Figge: Davenport Bank & Trust Co., Davenport, Iowa

THE
AMERICAN
COWBOY

HAROLD McCRACKEN

Doubleday & Company, Inc.
Garden City, New York
1973

ACKNOWLEDGMENTS

I am indebted to my wife Angelyn, who has always aided me, proofread my manuscripts and galleys, and been my kindest critic. Also to my secretary, Mrs. Joyce Mayer, who grew up among Wyoming cowboys and was a rodeo rider until a serious accident ended that career. To my father Jim McCracken (1860–1941), pioneer newspaper publisher and feature writer who roamed the West from the early 1880s to 1897 and who gave me my earliest interest in cowboys. To the many books published through the past hundred years dealing with cowboys and the cattle industry, which gave me the desire to attempt the present book. To Charlie Dye, John Clymer, and José Cisneros, the fine artists who made pictures especially for this book. For permissions and courtesies granted by Paul R. Melcher, Executor of the Edward Borein Estate; Mr. and Mrs. James F. Ash, Executors of the Frank Tenney Johnson Estate; John C. Traphagen, Executor of the W. R. Leigh Estate; Mrs. Verna Stough Belden, Executor of the Charles J. Belden Estate; V. O. Figge and the Davenport Bank and Trust Company; the Exchange Bank and Trust Company, Dallas; Mrs. Ruth Koerner Oliver; Paul Frison; Herbert O. Brayer; Harold G. Davidson; Dr. H. I. Burtness; William D. Weiss; William E. Weiss; L. B. "Bud" Maytag; Ted DeGrazia; Jack Bartfield; Joseph M. Roebling; William Magee; Fred Rosenstock; Jack Richard, for his photography; and especially to Harold Kuebler, for his valuable guidance and assistance in the difficult preparation of this book.

Harold McCracken

ISBN 0-385-04938-2
Library of Congress Catalog Card Number 72-76189
Copyright © 1973 by Harold McCracken
ALL RIGHTS RESERVED
PRINTED IN THE UNITED STATES OF AMERICA

FIRST EDITION AFTER THE LIMITED EDITION OF 300 COPIES

CONTENTS

"The Trail Boss"–EDWARD BOREIN–Hammer Galleries, N.Y.

ILLUSTRATIONS

Color

Black and White

"There ain't no horse
That cain't be rode
and
There ain't no man
That cain't be throwed"

—*"Wild Horse" Bill*

"The Classic American Cowboy"–FREDERIC REMINGTON

Chapter 1

NOT FOLKLORE
BUT HISTORY

Glamorous incidents in the human pageantry of history, as they slip farther and farther into the limbo of the past, sometimes take on an aura that seems more folklore than fact. Such misinterpretations are often influenced by writers and the creators of other media intended primarily for popular entertainment. Using historical characters and backgrounds, they exaggerate the sensational at the expense of the more credible. This has been particularly true in the case of the American cowboy.

The American cowboy rode quietly and unobtrusively upon our western scene, at a time when the broad frontier was just beginning to react to the coming of the white man's civilization. The cowboy played an important role in that important historic transition in the wilderness. It is difficult to say just when our cowboy was born, or when he died. His life was brief, in the manner in which the annals of man are recorded. Yet his epitaph is deeply engraved on the pages of our national history; and his story is widely known to legions and generations of young and old throughout the earth. He is recognized as the last of a long line of cavaliers, although he is probably better known today than the knights of King Arthur's Round Table, or the Spanish *conquistadors,* who brought to America the cowboy's horse and the cattle on which the economy of our western empire was built. He was generated out of a miscellany of men who were attracted to the frontier in search of adventure, and who came from nearly every type of family background, religion, and nationality. He became joined into a close fraternity of bravely flamboyant men, highly secular and as deeply devoted to their ways of life as the monks of Athos; yet they were as American as Fourth of July or apple pie.

The ancestral background of the cowboy goes back beyond the earliest recorded accounts of the human race. No one knows for sure when the first wild horses or cattle were captured and domesticated for the use and as chattel of their captors. Through many centuries of peace and warfare men of many races have utilized both horses and cattle for numerous purposes other than purely pastoral or economic benefit. From the earliest days of the pagan hordes on sturdy little Mongolian horses, and European knights in burnished armor, men on horseback have provided many of history's most exciting and colorful episodes. Jousting and other tournaments of sport and mortal combat between spirited adversaries were long accepted as popular games as well as for settling the most serious matters on a field of honor. There was a time in early Rome and Andalusia when bull fighting was as popular as football is in the United States today, and practically every nation has had its own form of equestrian feats and conquests. But of all the men on horseback, the American cowboy has gained the most widespread popular image, and that image will probably outshine the others in the future.

The first horsemen to handle herds of cattle in America were the early Spanish *vaqueros* in Mexico, following the introduction of horses and cattle onto this continent. As cattle-raising spread northward into present Arizona, California, Texas, and elsewhere, varying regional characteristics were developed among men and animals. It was, however, the cattle herders on the wide-open grasslands of the northern plains of present Wyoming and Montana that have become the recognized prototype of the American cowboy that is today known throughout the earth. The whole era of the Wyoming-Montana cowboy, which extended roughly from about 1870 to 1910, was made popular through the wide exposure given by the works of such accomplished artists as Frederic Remington and Charles M. Russell, and the writings of such as Owen Wister, Theodore Roosevelt, and others. This has been carried on abundantly through the years by an unending parade of artists, writers, playwrights, and moviemakers. All this has contributed to the image of the cowboy.

Civilization moved rapidly in upon the cattlemen's domains on the wide-open ranges, until the old days of cowboys and great herds were crowded behind the inescapable curtain of things gone forever. One of the last surviving regions of that rugged and exciting era in our history was in Wyoming. Here there were large expanses of semi-arid prairie that furnished suitable grazing for cattle, as it previously had for the great herds of buffalo. The skimpy, rock-filled Wyoming soil was less attractive to farming than that in other areas. In Montana and other parts of the northern plains, for example, the fertile, wide-spreading buffalo prairies were ideal for the expansive wheat growing enterprises that successfully exist today. So it was that Wyoming remained truly cattle country longer than elsewhere; and one of the last lingering vestiges of the old-time era was the Big Horn Basin in the northwestern part of the state. At the western edge of the basin and alongside the Rocky Mountains is the town of Cody, near the eastern entrance of Yellowstone National Park — which is also the present writer's hometown. As early as the 1870s, the famous frontiersman William F. "Buffalo Bill" Cody selected this place to be his final home; for even at that early date he felt it would be one of the last places to succumb to the onmarch of civilization. Here he had his own four hundred thousand-acre cattle ranch; here he spent his last days of retirement from the tours with his Wild West show; and a large part of that same sprawling acreage is still operated as a cattle ranch, although on quite a different basis than it was in the old days. And also today, it is not an infrequent sight on the wide three-block-long main street of the town that bears the old

"*Roped*"–EDWARD BOREIN

frontiersman's name to see one or two of the old-time cowboys—long retired from riding bucking broncos, but still clearly remembering what the era of the big herds and the cattle barons was really like.

Distinctive as were the cowboys of the northern plains, they inherited practically all of their basic methods of handling cattle, their gear, and even the lingo they used, from the Spanish-Colonial Texas *vaqueros*. Even the name "cow-boy" is supposed to have originated in the Texas cattle country, before there were any herds on the northern plains. After Texas had become a state of the Union in 1845, a considerable number of non-Spanish people settled there from Louisiana, Mississippi, and other southern states east of the Mississippi River. When the Civil War broke out, most of the able-bodied men joined the Confederate Army. Many of these families lived in the rural areas and had ranches on which it was normal to have a considerable number of Spanish longhorn cattle. The longhorns had become so numerous that nearly every ranch had as many as they could handle. When the men left for war, the handling of these family cows and beef cattle was of necessity turned over to the boys who were not old enough to join the Army. This was exciting work for the Texas youngsters, who took to the task with youthful enthusiasm. There were a large number of them, and it was only natural that they should become known as the "cow-boys." By the end of the Civil War they had greatly matured in the press of their man-sized duties, and had become quite adept in handling the obstinate and often pugnacious longhorns. It was shortly after the end of the war that Texans began rounding up their surplus cattle to be trailed to waiting markets in the North, and many of these war-created "cow-boys" were enlisted to help handle the trail herds. A goodly number of these young Texans decided to stay "up North," where prospects for a future were more

"The Trail Herd"–EDWARD BOREIN

promising; and they not only became instructors of the cattlemen on the northern plains, but gave the name of cowboy to their northern counterparts.

The factual story of the American cowboy is an important part of the history of the Old West and the taming of the wilderness. It is true that not all cowboys were paragons of gentility, heaven forbid! It is also true that they were normal human beings and on occasion visited the nearest cowtown, where they indulged with enthusiasm in all the diversions and iniquities that these places had to offer. Nor was it infrequent for them to get into trouble, and sometimes it was belligerently serious trouble. This is the aspect of their life that the fallacious fiction writers and Hollywood moviemakers have unreasonably magnified to the extent of giving a misleading impression of the real character of the cowboy. The cowtowns were generally an inconvenient distance away; and these men didn't make enough money to go there often. It is as unfair to mark them as trouble-seeking, hard-drinking, trigger-happy hellions as it would be to mark all of the Madison Avenue advertising men as commercial carpetbaggers.

In considering the cowboy in his day, one should keep clearly in mind that the West was still a very rough and raw place in which to live, and his job was the most demanding to be found, even on the frontier. The Indians had not as yet conceded their rights to the white man. In most places there was no law, except that which was created by those who on occasion decided to take such matters in their own hands. The Army tried to play policeman, jury, and judge, although it had more than could be taken care of in Indian troubles. Where there were sheriffs, courts, and jails, these were far apart, communications and transportation were slow, and justice was often controlled to suit powerful local interests. That is why the vigilantes were organized. Carrying arms, and the ability to use them, was a necessity in most areas; and this was not entirely because of hostile Indians or dangerous predatory animals. In those days the West was a good place for a fugitive from justice in some eastern state to become lost to his past and live as another person; and some of these became cowboys. There were also bona fide badmen who withdrew from holding up stagecoaches or wagon trains and decided to join a cattle outfit. But most of these sought the easier life with a mining or railroad construction crew, or in one of the little towns that had sprung up around the trading posts, overland stage stations, and army posts. Furthermore, the cowboy outfits had their own ways of ridding their groups of the unfit and undesirable.

There were no particular requirements to becoming a cowboy, except being physically able, and compatibility to becoming a member of the group. It mattered not whether he had gone to Harvard (which some had) or if his family lived in a big-city tenement or the house of the lord of a manor, or whether his hometown was Chicago, Dusseldorf, or San Antonio. Acceptance was invariably on a probation basis. A primary requirement was a natural or easily acquired ability to ride and handle a fractious horse, and to use a lasso. If the newcomer happened to be a particularly good camp jester, or had a good repertoire of funny or wild stories to tell around the campfire, that was sometimes enough to get him accepted, and given an "old lady" horse to carry him on "night-hawk" or other menial duty. Charlie Russell, the famous Montana cowboy artist, was a self-styled poor rider and incapable of roping a calf that was sitting down, although he worked as a highly accepted cowboy for a good many years. There were other very demanding requirements. The cowboy had to have plenty of guts; be faithful and dependable under the most demanding or difficult of circumstances; be pugnacious when handling obstreperous cattle; and be able to take the strenuous life, in the blistering heat of summer, subzero blizzards of winter, windstorms, sandstorms, rain, spring torrents and flash floods, prairie fire, quicksand, long days and black nights of lonely monotony, handle stampeding cattle, drink alkaline water, and meet situations when hostile Indians or gun-toting rustlers appeared with unexpected suddenness. It was survival of the fittest, in the rawest meaning of the term. And not the least was living without the company of a good woman, or the enjoyments of having a home and a family to call his own. It may seem unreasonable that any man should desire or could long tolerate such a life as a chosen profession; and it is even more surprising that so many did. They punched no time clock for the daily beginning or end of each strenuous day; didn't know that Sundays were supposed to be days of rest; never dreamed of anything but a seven-day week;

"Moving the Herd"–W. H. D. KOERNER

or expected time off for Fourth of July or other holidays. And they did it willingly, for as little as thirty dollars a month. It was all this that gave the cowboy his unusual character, and why there has never been another breed of man quite like him.

Under ordinary circumstances they were quiet and amiable individuals. They varied in physical appearance. The classic cowboy was tall and slender, with good shoulders, thin waist, long legs, and a fanny as flat as a pancake; although some were short and stocky, or most anything in between. But all were very muscular and hard as nails. Some were better at some duties than others. In the big outfits there were generally men who could tame the wildest mustang fresh from a wild herd; others who could put a rope loop on any extremity of steer, calf, or horse, when both were going at a fast gait; and still others who completely understood the midnight temperaments and idiosyncrasies of most any bunch of cattle, and could lull them into peaceful repose with songs that they made up themselves and in voices that only a bunch of half-wild bovines might consider music. And yet for all their diversity they shared a common bond: They rode the range because it was the sort of life preferred above any other; and many of them followed it until they were all stove up with broken bones, or rheumatism, or just got to the place in life when it was too much to ride the hurricane deck of a bucking bronco.

Theodore Roosevelt gave his own appraisal of the cowboy as long ago as 1884, when he was still actively operating his cattle ranch on the Little Big Horn in Dakota. He had the following to say to a New York *Tribune* reporter: "The cowboys are a much misrepresented set of people. . . . I have taken part with them in roundups, have eaten, slept, hunted and herded cattle with them, and have never had any difficulty. If you choose to enter rum shops or go on drinking sprees with them, it is as easy to get into difficulty as it would be in New York, or anywhere else . . . and there are many places in our cities where I should feel less safe than I would among the wildest cowboys in the West."[1]

"The American Cowboy"—CHARLIE DYE

"Taurus the Bull"–TED DE GRAZIA–Signs of the Zodiac

Chapter 2

IN THE BEGINNING

Herds of wild horses and cattle of various kinds roamed over widely separated areas of Europe, Asia, and Africa a great many thousands of years back in the unrecorded periods of prehistoric times. Taurus the Bull and Equus the Horse have figured prominently in the history of nations since long before recorded history began. As long ago as one hundred thousand years, ancient man hunted these animals for food, clothing, and other of life's necessities, just as the American Indians hunted the bison less than three hundred years ago. The Old Stone Age people of Europe had devised their crudely fashioned stone-pointed spears to aid them in killing the larger but less-dangerous animals with whom they shared a struggle for existence. It was a long bridge from these ancient peoples to the mounted cowboys and great herds of cattle on our western plains, but they are all part of the same thread of history.

The European timetables and practices in man's early involvement in horses and cattle have been largely conjecture, based on much more skimpy data than we have had in America. Relatively substantial evidence representing the period around twenty thousand years ago, however, has been gained from pictographic scenes that were painted on the walls of habitation caves in northern Spain and southern France. The most celebrated of these are the Lascaux paintings in caves along the Dordogne, Vezere, and Dronne. It has been established that these represent periods of the Upper Paleolithic cultures, when Stone Age man shared his environment with such awesome beasts as the mammoth, wooly-haired rhinoceros, and cave bear, along with the wild horses and cattle. The long-horned cattle brought to Mexico by the Spanish *con-quistadors* in the early sixteenth century bear a marked resemblance to those depicted on the walls of the Lascaux caves. Presumably the Spanish longhorns had the same ancestral blood in their veins, dating back to the days when those primitive artists kept watch for game from the same caves on the high cliffs, and made sorties down into the green valleys to pit their strength and skill against the formidable long-horned "aurochs." From the bones that have been examined of this European ancestor of the longhorns that were trailed north from Texas in the nineteenth century, it is obvious that the ancestor was indeed a far more imposing and powerful creature, with a massive body and horns that spread more than eleven feet.

It was probably a long time after primitive man drew pictures on the walls of his cave dwellings, representing the wild horses and cattle he hunted, before *Homo sapiens* first conceived the idea of domesticating those animals. It could have been accomplished thousands of years before there were records of any kind to establish the fact. There could also have been great periods of time separating this historic event as it happened in various regions of the earth. There are a considerable number of nationalistic legends and epics of significant antiquity that have an interesting bearing on the subject, although these provide but small assistance in establishing dates. Furthermore, having been handed down verbally through untold generations, they have been repeatedly subjected to changes to suit each storyteller's fancy.

There is a Scandinavian folktale about a Frost Giant of the frosted mountains, who lived on the milk of a subservient gigantic cow. When this legendary bovine licked the frost on the rocky mountains for its own food, there men began to grow. In Persian lore there is a pretty pastoral story about the clouds drifting across the blue sky being the cattle of the gods, moving in search of greener pastures in which to feed. In India, there is an old legend in the Sanskrit language that relates that long ago a fair-skinned, beef-eating people came down to India from Persia, and were converted to be vegetarians because religious Hindus considered the cow as sacred and must never be killed for food. There are other tales from Irish, Nordic, and even Icelandic regions indicating somewhat more directly the use of horses and cattle-raising. They are all a far cry from the cowboy on our western plains; but they can still be considered as bits of ancestral lore.

Beginning around four thousand to five thousand years ago, the evidences of domestication of both horses and cattle become quite conclusive in the cultural records of the Greeks, Romans, Egyptians, Babylonians, and other contemporary civilizations. Decorations and hieroglyphic writings still surviving on the walls of

"Lascaux Cave Paintings"–French Government Tourist Office

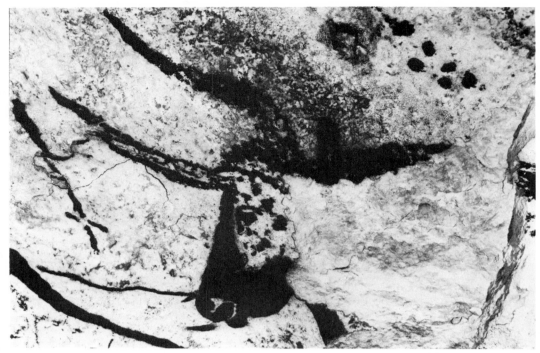

"Lascaux Cave Paintings"–French Government Tourist Office

ancient palaces, temples, and tombs frequently show cattle in a state of complete subservience, and horses hauling ornate chariots on expeditions of warfare and hunting.

There is much in the Old Testament that refers to "the cattle in the fields of the children of Israel"; the herds of domesticated cattle had by that time become a principal symbol of wealth and importance in Israel, Egypt, and elsewhere. Well known is the story of Abraham, who was born in 1996 B.C., who, according to the Book of Exodus, Chapter IX, was driven into Egypt because of the famine: "The Pharaoh took a liking to the beauty of his wife Sari, and took her into his family; but returned her, with a blessing of cattle and servants, so that when Abraham returned to Canaan he was much richer in cattle, silver, and gold." And in the Book of Zechariah there is a passage that is both prophetic and significant: "In the first chariot were red horses; and in the second chariot were black horses; and in the third chariot white horses; and in the fourth chariot were grizzled and bay horses . . . And the angel spoke, saying: There are the four spirits of heaven . . . and the black horses go forth into the north country; and the white go forth after them; and the grizzled go forth toward the south country; and the bay went forth . . . that they might walk to and fro on the earth."

In the Scriptures and other ancient writings, the term *catel* (cattle) and the Late Latin *capitale* signified all classes of livestock, including not only bovines but also horses, donkeys, sheep, goats, and in some regions including swine. The word was synonymous with wealth, and in its wider meaning as *chattel* or all kinds of worldly property. The bovines later came to be known as *ox* or *oxen,* from the *auroch,* its prehistoric ancestor. Continuing in this vein, after the introduction of metal coinage in ancient Greece, the new method of exchange commemorated the old by being stamped with the image of an ox. Thus the connection between cattle and coin left its permanent mark on the language of Europe in the Latin word *pecunia,* retained in its English derivation *pecuniary,* which refers to most anything relating to money.

The deep importance of cattle in ancient times is shown in numerous forms of the culture and mythology of nearly every part of Europe and Asia; and a good many of these have survived. "Taurus the Bull," the second sign of the Zodiac, is a two-thousand-year-old example.

Cattle, meaning specifically cows, have been one of the most important agents in the growth of early Old World civilizations, although man's association with the horse has through the centuries been one of conquests and has been flavored with far greater amounts of strenuous excitement. The advantages that the horse provided in warfare and hunting were quickly realized. A classic example is the case of our Plains Indians. We know the amazingly short period of time it required the Stone Age Indians of our West, who had no knowledge of the existence of white men, to capture the wild Spanish horses and completely adapt them to the needs of hunting the buffalo and in warfare against other tribes. Equally impressive is the sudden and great advancement the horse made in the whole culture of the American Indians. In Europe and Asia, at a much earlier period, the horse became of even greater importance to much larger nations, engaged in wide-scale conquests. Genghis Khan, the twelfth- and thirteenth-century Mongol ruler, could never have become the conqueror he was without his legions of warriors mounted on their comparatively small horses.

According to accredited authorities, the horse family has been an extensive and varied one, with ancestry going back as much as seventy million years, both in America and Europe. There was a period, about thirty million years ago, when the small (twenty-four inches high) three-toed horse was abundant on the same areas of present Wyoming where the nineteenth-century cowboys and big cattle herds held forth. For some unknown reason all the horses in America became extinct, although members of the family continued to survive and prosper in Europe, Asia, and Africa. In fact, there became about as many or more types of horses as there were humans, with even greater physical differences and temperaments. After domestication these differences became accentuated by man's crossing and selective breeding, training, and adapting to specific duties, through long lines of generations.

The earliest recorded reference to the domesticated horse in the British Isles was by Julius Caesar, after his second invasion of Britain in 54 B.C. On that occasion he led five legions and two thousand cavalry. But the British prince Cassivellaunus, with his war chariots, harassed the Roman columns to such an extent that Caesar had to withdraw from Britain; and in Caesar's own written account of the expedition he paid high tribute to the British horses and the skill with which they handled the war chariots. However, after the occupation of the country in about the first century by the Romans, their cavalry horses were crossed with the native mares, strengthening the breed, from which better Roman remounts were procured.

The period of the Norman conquest of Britain in 1066 marks another important stage in the development of the British horse, due to the fresh and stronger blood that was introduced. The horse of the Norman leader, William the Conqueror, is reported to have been of Spanish breed, although the invading forces had horses of many varieties, all of which added improvement to the native stock. It was also about this

"*The Babylonians—Persepolis Stairway*"–Oriental Institute, Univ. of Chicago

time, or shortly afterward, that a considerable number of stallions from Spain (probably Andalusians) and Barbs from Morocco were imported into Britain as well as other European countries. And of course the many thousands of men who participated in the Crusades at the end of the eleventh through the thirteenth centuries had a great influence on the development of the nonagricultural horses throughout all Europe, in fact the whole civilized earth. Up to that time there is very little evidence that horses were used for agricultural purposes—a role that seems to have been left to oxen.

The history of the horse is a long one. A good many scholarly volumes have been devoted to various phases of the subject. Our interest here, however, is primarily in the horses that were brought to America in the early part of the sixteenth century by the Spanish *conquistadors*. These were the first modern domesticated horses introduced into North America, and it was this original stock that provided the beginning for the horses on our great western plains. They were the ancestors of the many large herds of wild mustangs that spread northward much farther than the Spaniards who imported them. It was from those wild herds that the many Indian tribes obtained their horses, even before the red men knew that Europeans existed. It was also from this original stock that the American cowboys were provided their riding mounts.

These first horses in America presumably were of Andalusian origin; and probably their ancestry went back, in part at least, to the same type of wild horses shown in the Lascaux cave paintings on pages 20 and 21 of this book. However, it is known that even the Spanish Andalusian horses had undergone infusions of other types of horses, long before the days of Cortes and Coronado.

Andalusia was invaded in about 516 B.C. by the Carthaginians; and in 27 B.C. the region became the Roman province of Baetina. In the fifth century it was overrun by the Vandals; and in 711 came the Moors, who ruled until 1492. The invaders, particularly the Moors, brought with them some of the finest horses of Arabia and North Africa, which by the time of Columbus were highly prized in Spain and Portugal. It was from this stock, although a mixture and probably not from the best horse families, that the Spanish *conquistadors* brought the first horses to America.

"Hernando Cortes"

Chapter 3

THE FIRST HORSES
IN AMERICA

In all the history of civilized man's wanderings over the face of the earth, in quest of new lands to explore or conquer, there is nothing that equals the early-sixteenth-century exploits of the Spanish *conquistadors* under the leadership of Hernando Cortes. Their landing on the coast of Mexico in mid-March of the year 1519, with sixteen horses, was only twenty-seven years after Christopher Columbus had completed his first voyage across the Atlantic; and it had not yet been learned whether the new discovery was only a group of small islands, or if a large continent existed. Today, Cortes and his followers are generally credited with being the first Europeans of record to land on the mainland of America, as well as bringing the first horses to the continent. The undertaking was, however, far from being a scientific exploratory expedition. It was an adventure of premeditated conquest; a search for rich plunder and treasure, and the horses were taken along as a cavalry to aid the foot soldiers in the pillaging of the native inhabitants whom the invaders hoped to subjugate and rule with whip and sword.

A footnote to the official chronicle recorded by a member of the expedition, however, establishes the fact that Cortes and his men were not the first Europeans to set foot on the mainland of America. Their planned landing place was the mouth of the Rio de Grijalva on the southeastern coast of Mexico. This river was named after a sea-going adventurer by the name of Juan de Grijalva, who had previously been there on one or more occasions and who carried on some highly profitable trading with the inhabitants of sizable villages just a short distance above the swampy mouth of the river. Cortes had become excited by the wild tales this trader had brought back, telling of the fabulous riches in the new country, considered of insignificant value by the foolish natives. Included in the romantic stories were reports of large cities farther into the interior, the streets of which were paved with gold, and great quantities of precious stones were stored like beans in baskets. It was this phantasmal new land that Cortes and his followers set out to conquer. But they knew nothing more about the unexplored region—whether it was another island, or part of a vast continent;

"A Spanish Caravel–Sixteenth Century"

whether or not the inhabitants would be defenseless, or if they might have legions of chariots and well-armed soldiers like the stories they knew of the invincible legions of the ancient Romans, or the Moors who had conquered Spain. These things Cortes and his comparatively small number of followers had no way of knowing, as the motley group of awkward, top-heavy Spanish caravels sailed toward their destination. When they landed, would they be swept back into the sea; or would they be overwhelmed and exterminated? Had Grijalva been telling the truth? Was there even a river such as he had described, and had they followed the directions correctly?

That the landing place was found as hoped is well confirmed by the detailed description of this and the rest of the adventures that was recorded by Bernal Diaz del Castillo, one of the adventurers who accompanied the expedition. It was he who compiled what became known as *"The True History of the Conquest of New Spain."* The original manuscript was kept by Diaz and taken with him to Guatemala, where he took up permanent residence. After his death a copy was made and sent to King Philip II of Spain, and it was published in 1632. The first translation was made in 1800. The most comprehensive and best translation, with an elaborate Introduction and Notes, was prepared by Alfred Percival Maudslay, M.A., Honorary Professor of Archaeology, National Museum of Mexico, and published in five volumes, London, by the Hakluyt Society, 1908, with reproductions of the original maps and diagrams. This was made "from the only exact copy of the Original Manuscript." It is from this source that the following brief but reliable account of the coming of the first horses to America has been drawn.

"There were eleven ships both great and small . . ." wrote Diaz of the expedition when it set out from the Port of Trinidad on the southern coast of Cuba, on the eighteenth of February 1519. Diaz was there to go with them, and he continues: "We numbered five hundred and eight, not counting the shipmasters, pilots and sailors, who numbered about one hundred. There were sixteen horses and mares . . . thirty-two crossbowmen and thirteen musketeers; four falconets (small cannon used in the 16th and 17th centuries) and much powder and ball."[2]

The horses and their owners were described in detail by Diaz, who referred to the horses as of Andalusian stock; and it is interesting to note the wide variations, as described by one who was there at the time:

"*Captain Cortes*   A vicious dark chestnut horse, which died as soon as we arrived at San Juan de Ulua.

"*Pedro de Alvarado* and *Hermando Lopez de Avila*   A very good sorrel mare, good both for sport and as a charger. When we arrived at New Spain, Pedro de Alvarado bought the other half share in the mare, or took it by force.

"*Alonzo Hernandez Puertocarrero*   A gray mare, a very good charger which Cortes bought from him with his gold buttons.

"*Juan Valasquez de Leon*   A very powerful gray mare which we called "La Rabona" (the bob-tailed), very handy and a good charger.

"*Cristoval de Olid*   A dark chestnut horse, fairly good.

"The First Cattle in America"

"*Francisco de Montejo* and *Alonzo de Avila*   A parched sorrel horse, no use for warfare.

"*Francisco de Morla*   A dark chestnut horse, very fast and very easily handled.

"*Juan de Escalante*   A light chestnut horse with three white stockings, not much good.

"*Diego de Ordas*   A gray mare, barren, tolerably good, but not fast.

"*Gonzalo Dominquez*   A wonderfully good horseman, a very good dark chestnut horse, a grand galloper.

"*Pedro de Trujillo*   A good chestnut horse, all chestnut, a very good goer.

"*Moron,* a settler at Bayamo   A dappled horse with stockings on the forefeet, very handy.

"*Baena,* a settler at Trinidad   A dappled horse almost black, no good for anything.

"*Lares,* a very good horseman   An excellent horse of rather light chestnut colour, a very good goer.

"*Ortiz* the musician and *Bartholome Garcia,* who once owned a gold mine   A very good dark horse called "El Arriero" (the muleteon, carrier). This was one of the best horses carried in the fleet.

"*Juan Sedeno,* a settler at Havana   A chestnut mare which foaled on board ship."[3]

Diaz wrote an interesting footnote to the above, which reads: "This Juan Sedeno passed for the richest soldier in the fleet, for he came in his own ship with the mare, and a negro and a store of cassava bread and salt pork, and at that time horses and negroes were worth their weight in gold, and that is the reason why more horses were not taken, for there were none to be bought."

After considerable difficulties and delays the fleet arrived at the mouth of the Rio de Grijalva on the twelfth of March 1519, and all the sailors, soldiers, and expeditionary force were landed at the Cape of Palms. The river, the river banks, and the mangrove thickets were swarming with hostile Indians. It was learned that more than twelve thousand warriors were assembled at the town a short distance up the river, all prepared to make war on the intruders. Cortes advanced his force upstream, and after a day of bitter fighting the town was stormed and taken. Cortes then went through the ceremony of theoretically taking possession of the entire country in the name of the Crown of Spain. The Spaniards had been greatly outnumbered, and a good many of the soldiers had been wounded by the arrows and spears of the Indians in spite of the protective armor and helmets the Spaniards wore. It was later learned that an even larger force of Indian warriors was being hurriedly assembled from the surrounding country to wipe out the invaders.

In temporary control of the town, which Diaz calls Tobasco, the Spaniards prepared to continue their conquest. Cortes gave orders for *all the horses to be landed from the ships.* Thus, the first horses to land on the mainland coast of the North American continent were brought ashore on either the fourteenth or fifteenth day of

"Spanish Conquistador—Sixteenth Century"—JOSÉ CISNEROS
"Riders of the Border"

March 1519. Diaz's account is a little vague as to the exact day the landing of the horses was made. That those sixteen horses were to be the first cavalry to participate in warfare in the New World was only one prophetic indication of things to come in the distant future. Little could any of those *conquistadors* realize what a tremendous impact the bringing of horses to this continent was eventually to mean. The tremendous cultural development of hundreds of thousands of the unknown primitive Indian tribes of both North and South America was to become only part of the benefit. One of the richest benefactors was to be the whole cattle industry of the American West. In fact, that adventurous early-sixteenth-century landing of those first horses on the primitive southeastern coast of Mexico was to become one of the most significant incidents in the exploration and development of the American continent.

The horses had been confined for nearly a whole month in the lower decks of the caravels, which were so top-heavy they rolled and pitched even in a calm sea, and the feed had probably not been too good. It was hardly the best of preparatory conditioning for any horses to be pushed into battle against a horde of yelling, spear-throwing, and arrow-shooting wild Mexican Indians. But before the horses had time to get the kinks out of their sea legs, they were ridden into the very critical engagement. Such a large number of Indian warriors had been assembled that Diaz reports "they outnumbered us about three hundred to one." The battle was going rather badly for the Spaniards until the little cavalry of lame and sea-weary horses made their dash upon the scene. "The Indians thought the horse and its rider were all one animal," states Diaz, "for they had never seen horses up to that time; and the hordes of native warriors were so startled they were thrown into fright, and they retreated in great disorder." Thus ended in victory the first cavalry charge on the American continent.

Cortes and his followers went on to conquer all of Mexico. Wherever they went it was with a ruthlessness that hardly bears comparison. It is interesting to note that a common final comment to the reports of several of the most critical of the Spanish *conquistadors'* engagements was: "After God, we owed the victory to our horses."

The "age of horses" in America is generally reckoned as beginning with the landing of those sixteen horses and mares on the southern part of the east coast of Mexico by the Cortes expedition. It is possible, however, that these were not the first to set hoof on the continent. There are a good many unheralded priorities in the field of exploration. The fact that Cortes followed the Spanish trader Juan de Grijalva is an example. But who ever heard of Juan de Grijalva? That Leif Ericsson and his Norsemen crossed the Atlantic to the New World some five hundred years before Columbus "discovered" America has been pretty well established. There is belief by some recent investigators that the Norsemen brought both horses and cattle with them; but if they did, none survived to permanently propagate their breed in the New World. It is also possible that horses may have been taken to Florida from nearby Cuba prior to the Cortes expedition; if so, these apparently did not survive.

From the time that Columbus returned from his first voyage, the word spread rapidly, and with that magic Spanish romantic exaggeration it became believed throughout Spain that the newly discovered land was one of gold and riches that awaited all who would go there and take them. When the stories of Cortes' conquests came home, the excitement flowed with renewed and confirmed belief. Now there were no doubts. There was indeed a real pot of gold at the end of the rainbow where it came down to earth in the new land across the sea. More and more ships left Spanish and Portuguese ports and sailed over the horizon into the west. These were large and small, good and bad, some ill-equipped and poorly manned. Most of them made the passage safely, although a good many never made a landfall.

As Spain gained a *pied-à-terre* in the New World and the official reports were sent back by Cortes and others, there was such repeated emphasis put on the importance of the role the horse had played in the conquests, especially in those incidents when the Spaniards were greatly outnumbered, that Emperor Charles V made it virtually mandatory for every new expedition to take a quota of both horses and mares. This policy was continued by his son Philip. In the year 1535, a Don Alonzo Louis de Lugo was granted permission by Charles V to lead an expedition to the New World, and as part of the terms of the agreement "bound himself to take fifteen hundred men and two hundred horses as well as mares for breeding purposes."[4]

Columbus, on his second voyage in 1493, had taken fifteen horses and ten mares to the island of Hispaniola; and nearly all of the other following expeditions with

"First of His Race"–FREDERIC REMINGTON

ships large enough had taken horses along for both military and breeding purposes, and these had thrived and multiplied on the islands.

Not all of the large and well-equipped expeditions escaped ultimate disaster. Most notable among these was one that set sail on June, 27, 1527 under the leadership of Panfilo de Narvaez. He had a flotilla of five large, ornate but awkward caravels, with broad bow, high, narrow poop, and large, decorated sails. There were some six hundred men and eighty horses on board. The objective was the conquest of all "Florida," which at that time was believed to extend from present Florida to Mexico. The official treasurer of the expedition was a young Spaniard by the name of Cabeza de Vaca.

The Narvaez expedition made the Atlantic crossing safely, and stopped at the Cuban town of Trinidad, as was customary, to take on fresh water, supplies, and sometimes more horses. It was at Trinidad that a large number of Narvaez' men deserted, as was sometimes the case, to remain under the palm trees and enjoy the lazy Caribbean atmosphere. But those warm, enchanting zephyrs wafting across the calm turquoise sea are a lot like the beautiful mulatto descendants of the Spanish *conquistadors,* for they could suddenly change into the wrath of a tropical hurricane; and the caravels of the Narvaez expedition were suddenly lashed and almost destroyed before they could be sailed away from the coast.

The sorely depleted expedition finally landed on the western coast of Florida in the vicinity of the present city of Tampa. Only forty-two of the eighty horses remained alive, after more than two months in the holds of the gyrating caravels. The equine survivors were so lean, weak, and bruised they could hardly walk. The expedition struggled inland, through swamps and rattlesnake-infested palmetto plains in search of the cities of fabulous treasure and beautiful women. Constant hardship and disappointment multiplied into catastrophe and tragedy for both men and horses. Soon all that remained of the once-proud expedition were four survivors, among them Cabeza de Vaca. Caught in the arms of a violent storm, half drowned, practically naked, and without food, they were cast up on the sandy shores of the Gulf of Mexico in the vicinity of present Galveston, Texas. Their barefoot journey across present Texas to Mexico City, arriving on July, 24, 1536 after eight long years of travail, is one of the classic sagas of man's struggle for survival in the wilderness. No four civilized men ever traversed so much of the earth that was entirely new to mankind, under such extraordinary circumstances, and came home to tell about it.

The expedition under Hernando de Soto fared somewhat better, although all their hopes ended in disappointment. Like the Narvaez expedition, they landed at Tampa Bay on the western coast of Florida. It was in May 1538; they had about 200 horsemen and 560 foot soldiers. They too set out through the swamps and palmetto plains. The depleted force reached the Mississippi River in 1541, and spent the following year on the plains to the west. De Soto died in June 1542, and was buried in the great river he discovered. The route of the survivors traversed what are now the states of Arkansas, Oklahoma, and Texas, and finally southward to Mexico. Some historians believe the De Soto expedition provided original stock for populating the plains with horses. It is plausible to assume that some of the De Soto horses may have escaped; and if they had offspring there is no reason why they could not have further propagated and developed healthy herds of wild horses, although there is no substantial evidence to support this possibility.

The undertakings of the Spanish *conquistadors* were far more military than pastoral. Their basic motive was to satisfy an insatiable lust for gold and other riches, a harvest to be gathered by fair means or foul, or by force, in any form the situation required. But cattle had for centuries been considered essential to the permanent development of new areas, where people were intent on settling down to establish homes and raise families and future generations. The raising of cattle and other livestock was introduced on the island of Hispaniola by Columbus on his second voyage in 1493. (Columbus was not a *conquistador*.) The first cattle were taken to Mexico only two years after Cortes began his conquest. It is Gregorio de Villalobos who deserves credit for taking these cattle to the mainland. Below the high poop, in the belly of his rolling caravel, tied to stanchions to avoid broken legs, was a small group of calves that had been born on Hispaniola. The exact number has been in dispute, although it was apparently six heifers and one young bull. They were of the Andalusian breed that came to be known as Spanish longhorns. With the horses that had preceded them, they were the initial vanguard that was destined to bring to the American continent an influence that was to shape the history of the most powerful nation on earth, and a wealth that was to far exceed all the gold and other riches acquired by all the *conquistadors.*

Following the arrival of this small group of young longhorns in Mexico in 1521, cattle raising began and actively increased. Under the personal efforts of Cortes and Antonio de Mendoza, the first viceroy and colonial administrator of New Spain, the new industry rapidly expanded. The first herders of cattle on the continent were the strongest and most usable of the native men, who were spared from groups of recalcitrant local inhabitants who were slaughtered. These were pressed into slavery and sold, after they were branded with a hot iron on the cheek with a "G," signifying *guerra* (war).

By the time Francisco Vásquez Coronado organized his historic expedition of 1540, the herds of horses and cattle had increased to a surprising extent. The large amount of information we have on this ill-fated undertaking is due to the chronicle of Pedro de Castaneda. A copy of the original Spanish manuscript, together with a translation and interpretation by George Parker Winship, is assembled in the voluminous Fourteenth Annual Report of the Bureau of Ethnology of the Smithsonian Institution, 1892–93. It is largely from this source that the following abbreviated account has been drawn.

The Coronado expedition was assembled at the town of Compostela, in northern Mexico. Viceroy Mendoza had come to review the column as they began the great conquest of the fabled cities of Cibola and Quivira, and the supposedly rich kingdoms to the north. The expedition started on February 23, 1540, and the chronicler describes it as the most brilliant company of *conquistadors* to carry the flag of Spain in search of new lands to conquer. General Coronado wore magnificent gilded armor and a plumed helmet. He had an honor guard of approximately three hundred mounted gentlemen of high birth, arrogant scions of Castile, who gloried in their noble birth. The young cavaliers curbed their spirited horses from the large stock farm of the Viceroy, and each rider had a reserve of several mounts attended by servants, who followed in the rear. Each rider held his lance erect, while his sword and other weapons hung in their proper place at his side. Some were arrayed in coats of mail, polished to shine like that of their general. Others wore iron helmets or vizored headpieces of tough bullhide. The footmen carried crossbows or harquebuses, while some were armed with great swords and shields. They started out with banners flying. There were upward of a thousand servants and followers, black men and red men, leading the spare horses, driving the pack animals, bearing the extra baggage of their masters, or herding along the large droves of "big and little cattle," of oxen and cows, sheep and even swine, which had been collected by the viceroy to afford fresh food for the army on its march. There were more than a thousand horses in the cavalcade, besides the mules, loaded with camp supplies and provisions, and carrying half a dozen pieces of light artillery, *pedreros* (swivel guns of the period).

Everyone was eager and enthusiastic at the start. But the cattle could not be hurried, and animals and men were so heavily laden they had to go slowly. The black men and red men who attended the spare horses were not accustomed to handling such spirited animals and had difficulties with them; and the crossing of rivers presented great problems. Even the auxiliary force of more than eight hundred Mexican Indian allies, and the large numbers of pack horses, mules, cattle, sheep, and swine each added individual problems and complications.

Before the expedition reached the first of the Seven Cities of Cibola, it had spent nearly five months, strung out, disorganized, discouraged, desperately short of food, weary, and sadly disenchanted with the whole affair. They had abandoned cattle and lost horses. They had to fight their way into the first village of Cibola. None of the invaders were killed by the Zuni defenders, but a few had been wounded by arrows, and most had suffered bruises from being hit by stones thrown by the Indians. Even Coronado was twice knocked from his horse by large stones dropped on him from upper floors of the pueblos. Worst of all was the fact that there was no rich treasure of any kind in all of Cibola to reward the *conquistadors* for all their trials and tribulations.

But the expedition pressed on, with always more of the same, until they were caught in the snowstorms and bitter cold of the first winter, in the Albuquerque-Bernalillo area. Here they set up the first winter quarters, and encountered continual harassment from the local Indians. In one of the attacks the Indians stampeded the horses and drove a large number away.

The story of the Coronado expedition is a long, exciting, and frustrating saga of adventure. Still determined to reach the fabled city of Quivira, the dwindling cavalcade pressed on. For two years they wandered over the mountains and out across the wide buffalo plains, exploring what is today the states of New Mexico, Texas, Oklahoma, Kansas, and Nebraska. They finally reached what they believed to be Quivira. As Coronado himself wrote: "The guides had pictured it as having stone houses many stories high . . . but they were of straw." And there was no gold. The chief guide had his head cut off; and the ragged remnants of the once-proud Coronado expedition turned its weary way toward home. Before the end of the journey the disconsolate leader became so ill he had to be transported on a litter—empty-handed and with less than a hundred of the original expedition.

It is easily understood how many of the horses from the Coronado expedition were lost, strayed, or stolen during the numerous conflicts with the Indians, the long winters, and while wandering across the lush buffalo plains. The country was a natural habitat for horses, as it had for centuries been for the buffalo, deer, antelope, and elk. The Spanish horses that unquestionably escaped from the Coronado expedition could easily have been the original seed for the great herds of wild horses that spread northward across the entire extent of the Great Plains, to the tremendous benefit of nearly all the Indian tribes, and from which the American cowboy gained so many of the mounts he rode in the golden days of the cattle industry. However, the fact that Coronado, De Soto, and Cabeza de Vaca found no treasure of any kind, only primitive poverty, caused the Spanish *conquistadors* to lose interest in what is now our Southwest and to turn their conquests to South America and the more attractive coastal regions of California.

"The Coronado Expedition" – FREDERIC REMINGTON

"The Longhorns"–JOHN CLYMER–Harold McCracken Collection

Chapter 4

THE HORSE
TRAVELED FAST

The Spanish conquest of South America began surprisingly soon after Cortes landed in Mexico, and progressed with far greater rapidity than in North America. The same is true of the spread of the horse. The reason is quite obvious. Along the western coast of South America there was a highly developed Indian culture, much like that in Mexico. The Incas in Peru had imposing temples built of blocks of hewn stone and ruled over by potentates and high priests; the native women were attractive; there were large amounts of artifacts, and articles of personal adornment and public adoration, made of solid gold and silver, adorned with precious and semiprecious stones such as emeralds, amethysts, topaz, native diamonds, and pearls. These were the things the *conquistadors* had found in Mexico, but had not been able to find in any part of the regions to the north of Mexico or the Gulf. The information spread after the first explorers went down the coast in 1532; and caravels were hurriedly built in the bays on the Pacific coast to transport men and horses to the newly found lands. It was always a race to be the first, for it was they who generally reaped the richest harvest.

It has been pretty well established that the Spanish introduced the horse down the western coast of South America to Peru in 1532, and into present Chile and through the narrow Andes Mountains out across the pampas of Argentina, and into Uruguay and Paraguay before the middle of the sixteenth century. That was two centuries before the horse found its way northward through the present states of Wyoming, Montana, and the Dakotas; and this was not through any direct means provided by the Spanish, but by the animals' own peregrinations in self-propagated wild herds. Some cattle later followed down along the *conquistador* trail, although the herds on the pampas originated principally by ships crossing the South Atlantic from Spain and Portugal, possibly as early as 1535.*

*Dates on the spread of the horse in the Americas has been largely based on an extensive assemblage of information gathered by the staff of Princeton University Library's Department of Rare Books and Special Collections, under the direction of H. C. Rice, Jr., with such authorities as Edward Lacoque Tinker. This was in connection with an exhibition on "The Horsemen of the Americas and the Literature They Have Inspired," February 20 to April 10, 1953. A copy of the unpublished manuscript has been of special assistance to the present writer.

It can be seen, as a matter of comparison, that horse- and cattle-raising began on the pampas of southern South America a long time before it began on our northern plains; and it continued down there on a large and profitable scale long after it ended on our open range. In sections of Argentina, Uruguay, and Paraguay it still survives.

Not so many years ago, during a trip through South America, I saw much of the South American *gauchos* and their horses and cattle. In the back country of the Peruvian Andes I was introduced to the sort of horses the *conquistadors* rode on their early journeys into the country. They were rather small, woolly-haired animals, such as the Incas had been riding for four centuries; and they carried me easily up the perpendicular mountains to explore some ancient ruins. They were the finest of mountain climbing horses, but in every instance I found them absolutely saturated with a particular variety of fleas that seemed to consider a fair and thin-skinned Scotsman rider an opportunity for a feast of a lifetime. Whether or not the fleas had any relationship to the *conquistadors* and their horses, I had no way of learning, for I ended my field research on the subject as quickly as possible.

In northern Uruguay I was guest on a large and well-stocked cattle ranch that sprawled over a considerable area of grassy, palm-decorated pampas (*compo* they call it in Uruguay) on the border of Brazil. In Argentina I was guest of the famous heavy-weight prize fighter Luis Angel Firpo, "The Bull of the Pampas," on one of his several sprawling cattle ranches, a night and a day journey by train and auto from Buenos Aires. In both countries the cattle were in appearance very much like our own present

"Amigos"–EDWARD BOREIN

"A Mexican Vaquero" –FREDERIC REMINGTON

shorthorn varieties; and they were in beautiful condition, although requiring far less grazing acreage than in Wyoming. In Argentina there were miles and miles of the most lush clover I have ever seen, which produces the finest filet mignon on earth. In both places I had plenty of opportunity to observe the Spanish-speaking present-day *gauchos,* in their big baggy ankle-long bloomer pants; and I can attest to their skill in riding and handling cattle on horses that were as fine as ridden on any range. Even the 250-pound Firpo was an exceptional rider who had a string of his own personal mounts that were of necessity the strongest that could be found in Argentina, and he rode with the stirrups pulled up, like those of a jockey.

Both in Uruguay and Argentina I was feted in the evenings with an elaborate *esado* (barbeque of whole roasted lamb, chickens, blood sausage, etc.), which had required an all-day preparation by some of the tough, hard-riding, knife-carrying *gauchos.* While the two-hour-long outdoor feast was being enjoyed, along with plenty of fine wine, the cattle herders entertained us with guitar music and El Parydor folk songs, relating old-time Spanish sagas of romance and chivalry, celebrating love and tragedy, just as the traveling troubadors did in Spain long before the first *conquistadors* came to America. On one occasion I had young armadillo roasted in the shell, which Firpo had caught with his hands and brought in to be especially prepared for me.

As our own old-time cowboys were in the habit of doing, these *gauchos* occasionally went to town to have a little spree. They often took along their guitars, and sometimes their drinking led to impromptu contests in singing improvised songs celebrating their own conquests in love or war. Occasionally, so I was told, these singing contests of braggadocio became so intensified that they had to be settled with the long knives carried stuck inside their belts at the back. But on occasion I watched these *gauchos* dance the beautiful *perecon,* in groups of a dozen or more couples with attractive black-haired *señoritas*—a dance closely resembling our own graceful and quietly performed Colonial minuet. It was quite a contrast to anything ever seen in our cowboy land.

A deep-rooted hatred of the old-time Spaniard still survives in South America, particularly in the back country along the western coast and among those who have a goodly amount of Indian blood in their veins, for they remember the sword and the whip with which the *conquistadors* subjugated and ruled their ancestors. But even the llama-raising and -herding Incas of today, who are prosperous enough to afford a horse, are always proud to own one.

The importance of the horse to the early Spanish explorers was paramount. At the conclusion of his account of the Coronado expedition, Pedro de Castaneda had this to say: "Horses are the most necessary things in the new country, as they frighten the enemy most." However, it was as a means of transportation that the horse was most important. The relatively short time it took to explore the South American continent, literally from end to end, and conquer it at the same time, is made more

"Mexican Vaqueros Breaking a 'Bronc'"—FREDERIC REMINGTON

"*A Mexican Duel*"–FREDERIC REMINGTON

remarkable when one considers the sort of country the *conquistadors* had to traverse. It was a totally unexplored land which varied in extremes from tropical jungle to completely arid desert, interspersed with barren, rocky mountain ridges that were difficult to cross. In the Andes, in the relatively small elongated area of present Chile, there were no less than twenty mountain peaks that had to be circumvented that were as high or higher than anything in all North America. Some of those ancient Indian trails through the high passes, which are today used by pack-horse smugglers between Chile and Argentina, meander for miles and miles with not so much as a blade of grass to be found. Without the horse, the *conquistadors* could never have traveled as far or as wide as history has recorded they did. Even with the assistance of the horse, the Spanish faced the almost constant harassment of hostile Indians along the way. That not all of those early Spanish invaders survived their encounters with the Indians is mutely attested by a shrunken leather *conquistador* stirrup and the rust-encrusted remains of a Spanish dagger, now in my possession, which had been taken from the grave of an Indian who died about four hundred years ago near the end of one of the over-the-Andes trails in central Chile.

It must not be assumed that all of the Spaniards who came to America in the early days of conquest and colonization were satiated with only a desire for confiscation of treasure. The first ranch and stock-raising industry in the New World was planned and developed through the efforts of Christopher Columbus. The flotilla of ships that he guided across the Atlantic on his second voyage brought pastoral-minded men, and farm stock of all kinds for peaceful propagation on pioneer homesteads in Hispaniola. The industry prospered, and spread to Cuba and elsewhere. For a while the *conquistadors* were their best customers, although it was the beginning of horse and cattle ranching in America, and led to the great ranches of the era of cattle raising on the open ranges of our West.

Even Cortes and Coronado turned to stock raising after their more exciting adventures. Cortes was probably the first to put identifying brands on his cattle. The triple Christian cross with which he marked his stock was the forerunner of the myriads of recorded cattle brands that are still used on our western ranches. And it was Coronado who unintentionally was responsible for starting the first herds of wild cattle, which later supplied stock for commercial ranches. Early on his historic expedition in 1540 he abandoned at Sinaloa, in northwestern Mexico, an unknown number of the cattle being taken as food for members of the entourage. The slow-moving longhorns impeded progress and were difficult to control. Twenty-five years later, according to Paul I. Wellman in *The Trampling Herd* (1939), Francisco de Ibarra discovered thousands of their descendants running wild in the same area; and within a few decades great ranches were established in the province, one of them possessing so many cattle that it is reported to have branded thirty thousand calves in a year. It was here that probably the first *vaqueros* (Mexican cowboys) were used to handle cattle on a large scale.

Viceroy Antonio de Mendoza, who assisted Coronado in organizing his expedition, took early leadership in developing livestock raising in New Spain. He not only became active in importing horses and cattle for breeding purposes, but he also

"Vaquero"–EDWARD BOREIN

"Waving the Serape"–FREDERIC REMINGTON

encouraged the early colonists to get wives and settle down to pastoral pursuits. Further inducements were made by the King of Spain, in giving royal grants of huge areas of land to scions of noble families or other colonists who had performed favors to the new government. On some of these land grants the recipients built elegant *haciendas* in which they lived like feudal princes, developing large herds of cattle, and attended by many servants and mounted guards. The owners became known as *charros*, or gentlemen horsemen, while the hired herdsmen were called *vaqueros*.

The influx of Spanish pioneers into Mexico was similar to our own westward movement three hundred years later. The hope of finding new and better homes in a new land, with promise of a more abundant life, and flavored with a degree of adventure, has had a compelling appeal to men of all nationalities in all periods of history. Even domestic and wild animals seem to have the same urge to move ever onward, to enjoy the grass that always appears greener in a distant field. Thus, in Mexico the Spanish migration took root and then began to spread northward. To the south the country led into dense jungles, where the climate was too hot and humid.

From explorers to priests and pioneers, everywhere the Spaniards went the horse went with them. Although the *conquistadors* with all their flamboyant buccaneering faded into the past, the horse continued to prosper and increase in a prolific manner. They took naturally to the country, and in a remarkably short length of time herds of wild Spanish horses began spreading onto the grasslands of our western plains, as well as the broad pampas of South America.

"The Coming of Cattle to Texas"–JOSÉ CISNEROS–Harold McCracken Collection

Chapter 5

TREAD OF
THE LONGHORNS

Horses and cattle played such important roles in the story of our early West that it is almost impossible to think of the story without them. It is like trying to think of this country if the South had won the Civil War. English horses and Jersey shorthorn cattle were brought to Virginia and New England two or more centuries after Cortes, but the story was nothing comparable to that which followed the Spanish *conquistadors* and their Andalusian horses and longhorns. However, there is neither space nor necessity to trace here in chronological detail the spread of the Spanish horse or cattle through their various ramifications leading up to the era when the American cowboy made his brief ride across the pages of history. Interim details and dates are very interesting, although not all of the early ones are beyond dispute. In some instances the records are extremely scanty or there are none at all. Without a cursory abridgment, however, the purpose of this book would not be complete.

We know that Coronado abandoned cattle in Sinaloa in the northwestern part of Mexico, and that these tough and hardy longhorns propagated and prospered in the wild state. The same is true elsewhere. There is no reason to doubt the probability that some of these could have been taken farther north into Arizona, New Mexico, or beyond, considerably before the end of the sixteenth century. Because of the failure of the Coronado expedition there was comparatively little official interest in sending further military land ventures of conquest into the region to the north or northeast of Mexico. This left the area to the ecclesiastical and laymen pioneers, and further exploration in the north became largely diverted to the much easier way of traveling up the coast by ship.

Even before Coronado, the northward exploration of the Pacific coast began. Noteworthy are the voyages of Francisco de Ulloa, Hernando Alarcón, and Juan Rodriquez Cabrillo, as pioneers of the expeditions up the coast by ship. De Ulloa sailed north in the summer of 1539 in command of a small fleet that was sent out by Cortes. When these ships encountered the impassable shoals that extend southward from the mouth of the Colorado, unable to go farther, and without knowing what lay beyond, they turned back. The following spring Alarcón started out in command of another fleet of ships on the same course. He left Acapulco on May 9, 1540. When he reached the shoals and sandbars at the head of the Gulf of California, he took twenty men in two small boats and discovered the mouth of the Colorado River, on Thursday, August 26, 1540. Traveling up the river, they became the first men to navigate the Colorado. Upstream they met Indians who were aware of the fact that Coronado had visited Cibola, and the Spaniards learned there was a good trail by which one could travel overland between the two locations in about forty days. One of these Indians told the Spaniards that he had personally seen white men like themselves at Cibola, and that these white men had brought with them many cattle, and some of them rode on animals that ran very swiftly.[5]

Juan Rodriquez Cabrillo sailed north from the port of La Natividad on June 27, 1542, to explore the western side of the peninsula of Baja (Lower) California and to find out what land, if any, lay to the north. At the end of December he landed on one of the San Lucas Islands (off the coast from present Santa Barbara, California), where he died on January 3, 1543, leaving his chief pilot, Bartholome Ferrel, in command. Ferrel left the island of San Miguel, the smallest and northermost of these three islands, which he named Isla de Juan Rodriquez on January 29, and a little more than a month later the fleet reached 42° North, or close to the present southern boundary of Oregon. That he stopped along the way is evidenced by the report brought back that the Indians they encountered were aware that white men had visited the pueblo country, a long way to the south and back into the interior. As this was primarily a military expedition, everywhere they stopped the Spanish flag was ceremoniously planted to signify conquest of the country in the name of their King.[6] The expedition returned to Mexico without having found any rich treasure or cities to be conquered in the balmy and salubrious new land, although what they learned contributed to its future settlement.

Probably the strongest influences in Spanish development of the New World were the Catholic missionaries. The *padres* accompanied most of the early expeditions, sometimes following the overland explorations on foot. Representatives of either the Franciscan or Jesuit orders invariably followed later into the newly discovered regions. These missionaries were the real founding fathers of New Spain. Their primary purpose was to indoctrinate the Indians into their faith, but they were also responsible for bringing cattle, horses, sheep, goats, donkeys, and other domesticated stock into the parishes that they founded. Many of the priests were killed before they were able to establish friendly relationships with the Indians. But wherever the *padres* settled they created missions, taught the Indians to cultivate the land, and introduced the raising and handling of cattle. In most regions the local Indians took to riding horses with remarkable natural ability, which led to their becoming skilled *vaqueros*. The priests also taught the tanning of hides, rendering tallow, and the painting or carving of religious art for decorating the churches, which the Indians helped to build. The most desirable tracts of land in the region were appropriated by "squatter's rights," and in many instances these were large areas of fertile land. Through the years the

"A Mexican Longhorn"–FREDERICK REMINGTON

missions became centers of not only religious and cultural influence, but economic and political power as well. In some regions the influence of the Church grew to seriously challenge that of the local or federal government.

A number of the Spanish *padres* gained historic prominence. One of the most deserving of these was the Italian-born Jesuit priest Eusebio Francisco Kino. He came to be known as "the *padre* on horseback" and has often been referred to as "Arizona's first pioneer." He established missions in at least twenty places, scattered over a large part of the area known in the early Spanish era as Primera Alta, which today embraces the northwestern part of Mexico and a large part of southern Arizona. His main economic field of development in bringing civilized pursuits to the Indians was cattle raising, and he was certainly the cattle king of his era and region. And all this was accomplished more than half a century before the California missions were established. Father Kino was really the *padre* pioneer of the cattle industry in our whole West, for what he did primarily for the good of the Indians in that relatively small area spread to Texas and later throughout the great western plains.

Born in the town of Segno in northern Italy on August 10, 1645, Eusebio Francisco Kino came to Mexico as a Jesuit missionary in 1671; he died on March 15, 1711 at Magdalena, Sonora, Mexico, where he is buried. During the twenty-six years this dedicated man spent in New Spain he is credited with making more than forty long journeys on horseback through mountains and deserts, and probably covering more territory in the north country than any other individual of the period. One of these trips in the saddle was over a distance of twelve hundred miles, completed in seven weeks.[7] Then the priest had to ride back to the starting place. On another occasion, he explored the overland route from Arizona through the mountains and across the deserts to California and the Pacific coast, pioneering the way for the military expeditions and later the cattle drives from Texas.

Best known of the Kino-inspired missions is that of San Xavier del Bac, "The Dove of the Desert," a short distance south of the present Arizona city of Tucson. The *padre* officiated at laying the foundation of the original building in 1700. The present spectacularly beautiful mission building, which is the third or fourth rebuilding on the same location, was begun in 1785 and completed in 1795. It has been admired by hundreds of thousands of present-day tourists and is recognized as one of the Colonial architectural treasures of the Southwest. It is still used as a church by the large number of Papago Indians who live in the vicinity and who are still comparatively prosperous by means of the pastoral pursuits that Father Kino taught their ancestors and those of the other tribes in Primera Alta.

Father Kino was more than a *padre* on horseback, explorer, founder of many missions, and pioneer of the cattle industry in the Southwest. He was also an accomplished cartographer. The map that he made of Primera Alta, titled "Nuevo de la Nueva Navara," was published in 1705. That was a hundred years before the Lewis and Clark expedition completed its historic journey across the northern part of the United States. The map was made from Father Kino's personal explorations and travels on horseback. It covered the large area from the Pacific of the "Penisla de California" (Baja California) to "Albuquerq," Santa Fe, and the Pueblo of San Ildefonso in northern Nuevo Mexico (New Mexico). The rivers, mountains, locations of pueblos and Indian villages, churches, and even ranches were so completely and accurately recorded that the Kino map remained the accepted guide to the whole region until well into the nineteenth century.

Another Spanish missionary who made an important contribution to the development of the cattle industry in North America was the Franciscan missionary Father Junípero Serra, who accompanied the pioneer overland expedition from Mexico to California under the military leadership of Gaspar de Portola in 1769. Father Serra's purpose was basically the same as that of Father Kino. He realized that to civilize the Indians of California, the best approach was the establishment of missions, where they could be taught to practice agriculture, animal husbandry, hygiene, and handcraft. With these objectives in mind, Father Serra arranged to have the expedition take along as many head of livestock as possible; and when they arrived at the Bay of San Diego in July 1769 it was with about four hundred animals that had survived the journey. This was to begin the most successful as well as the most colorful early episode in the cattle-raising industry in North America. Out of this beginning was to develop the almost theatric "cattle on a thousand hills" of Southern California; the flamboyant California *vaquero;* and a romantic feudal aristocracy that has had no equal within the area that is today the United States.

The story of Father Serra is abundantly interesting, as is the story of the California cattle industry during the Spanish Colonial era. Southern California provided an ideal region for stock raising. The climate was as nearly perfect as could be desired

"Reata"–w. h. d. KOERNER–Courtesy Karl Obert

—warm the year round, with no blizzardy winters. There was an abundance of fine pasture lands and plenty of good water. The Indians took to herding, riding, and roping with such natural adaptability that they soon rivaled the Mexican *vaqueros*—which provided an abundance of cheap help. All that was necessary was to have some cattle and turn them loose in an area where they could be protected. The seed grew and multiplied into healthy herds, and the priestly masters prospered beyond the wildest expectations.

Hubert Howe Bancroft, in his classic *History of California,* has this to say about the beginning and rapid development of cattle raising in Southern California by the missions: "The first report of their work, in 1773, disclosed that 'Each mission had received 18 head of horned cattle and now has 38 to 47, or 204 in the aggregate; with 63 horses, 79 mules, 102 swine, and 161 sheep and goats at San Diego and San Gabriel alone.'"[8] And reporting on barely more than a decade later, the historian reports: "By letting nature take its course, the additional increase in eleven years at 9 of the 21 missions produced this census: 5384 cattle, 5629 sheep and 4294 goats. That was in 1784. By 1800 the estimate of all California's livestock totaled 74,000 cattle, 24,000 horses, 88,000 sheep, of which a large proportion belonged to the missions."[9] "When the missions reached the zenith of their prosperity in 1833, their own cattle numbered 424,000; sheep 321,500; and 62,500 horses and mules."[10] All this was a considerable number of years before the first trail drives of Texas longhorns began moving north to begin the development of the cattle industry on the open

"An Old-time California Cowboy"–FREDERIC REMINGTON

ranges of our northern plains. But it was at the time in California when the non-ecclesiastical big cattle ranches of the Spanish colonial feudal aristocracy were enjoying elegant full bloom.

From the time the first cattle were brought into California by Father Serra with the Portola military expedition, the region from San Diego north to the latitude of San Francisco had become a cattle raiser's paradise, and some very expansive ranches had been established. Nature took care of nearly all of the necessities, and the herds increased so rapidly that few of the owners knew how many head they could claim. Although the herds roamed in a semiwild state, the ranches were so large the cattle seldom wandered off the property. Even the lowliest employee could have a horse to ride if he asked for it; and beef to eat was as common as beans in Mexico.

"The Stranglers"–CHARLES M. RUSSELL

The Californians, as the Spanish-blooded *caballeros* were called, enjoyed themselves like true nobility. There were servants to do everything, except mount a fine horse and go dashing away. That was the *caballeros'* special enjoyment, and they excelled in it to a remarkable degree. To them a horseman and a gentleman of the first order were one and the same. But the *caballeros* were gentlemen in a class entirely separate from all others, spending their time riding from one fiesta or social pleasure to another, interspersing their leisure with sessions of gambling, horse racing, or the occasional diversion of gathering a few friends to ride out and rope a grizzly bear to be brought in alive for staging a fight to the death with the most pugnacious longhorn steer that could be found on the range. Sometimes grizzly and steer were each fastened at the end of the same rope or chain, to insure total destruction to one or the other.

Young ladies often rode in front in the saddle, gallantly supported by a gay young *caballero,* who sat behind. But the women lacked none of the proud horsemanship that was the hallmark of their aristocratic blood. They sometimes rode out to watch the bear-roping, and always were on hand when bear and bull met, to see which would survive. Wherever and whenever these fair ladies appeared to be seen by their admiring men, they were dressed in their elegant costumes made from the rich silks, damasks, and other fine fabrics brought to the California coast from China and India by Spanish galleons and Yankee four-riggers, returning for more hides to take back for trade. And the men, sometimes on special fiesta days, outrivaled their women in the most gorgeous costumes that horsemen ever wore—red-and-blue velvet jackets and pants, tightly fitted to accentuate a muscular physique and open down the sides to display the white linen underneath, and all trimmed in gold and silver filigree decoration, Spanish lace, and maybe some black pearls from the Gulf of California or semiprecious stones from South America or the Orient. They had first call on the Spanish and Yankee traders just back from the Far East, and there were always plenty of hides to use as barter.

It was only natural that a strong rivalry should develop and fester between the rich California *rancheros* and the much longer-established *padre*-controlled missions, from which nearly all the original cattle had been obtained. This finally came to a climax, with the wealthy ranchers using their political and financial influence. Historian Bancroft reports the results: "The severest blow to the missionary enterprise came with the enforcement of secularization in 1834. This policy of the recently established Mexican Republic purported to emancipate the natives and divide the mission lands among their neophytes, who, argue the authorities, were 'disgusted at having to support by their labor themselves, the *padre,* the government and the troops.' "[11] "To neutralize the effect of these harsh measures, the *padres* retaliated . . . by their wholesale slaughter of cattle in 1834, designed to bring them money for the sale of hides and tallow. . . . Outside contractors were hired to liquidate the livestock. . . . One contemporary reported that after a time nothing but the hides were saved . . . and from the hecatomb at San Gabriel there was alarm expressed at the possibility of a pestilence from the rotting carcasses."[12] One statistic cited by Bancroft indicates that in 1834 the port of Los Angeles received an estimated 100,000 hides and 250,000 pounds of tallow. The losses following this wholesale butchery are indicated in the official census of livestock holdings: In 1834 the total number of cattle at the twenty-one missions was 396,400; and by 1842 it had shrunk to 29,020. The disastrous results of secularization upon the missions added greatly to the already abundant prosperity of the *rancheros;* and a large number of new cattle ranches were established by the Californians. By 1840 there were more than five hundred of these. The "emancipated" Indians were incapable of taking advantage of their suddenly acquired self-determination. Many of them could do little better than seek employment in skinning off and dressing hides, and rendering tallow on the ranches of the Californians, or reverting back to the primitive life from which the *padres* had really emancipated them. For the *rancheros,* prosperity and more prosperity, took them into what came to be known as California's Golden Age. But even this began to wane when all life in California was radically changed by the discovery of gold. Within twenty years the population skyrocketed from about 15,000 to 750,000 commercially minded intruders of alien birth and an entirely different attitude from that of the luxury-loving Spanish Colonial *caballeros.* Thus the old days of the Spanish *padres,* and the Golden Age of the *rancheros,* slipped behind the dark curtain of an ever-changing history, at the time when even greater herds of Spanish longhorn cattle were moving north from Texas to establish another phase of cattle industry on our Northern Plains.

"Mexican Indian Vaquero"–FREDERIC REMINGTON–Kennedy Galleries, New York

"The Santa Fe Traders" —FRANK TENNEY JOHNSON

Chapter 6

THE WILD HERDS

The horse and the cow had for many centuries been used by man for various benefits, going far back into opaque prehistoric times. These animals had been brought to America at virtually the same time. Unknown to anyone, they were both destined to play very important roles in the undreamed-of great cattle industry in the still-undiscovered western plains of the still-unknown United States. Strangely enough, their equine and bovine descendants were to reach that ultimate journey's end by a rather circuitous route, including a long period of reversion to the wild state from which man captured and tamed them such a very long time before. They both reacted differently to returning to the primitive state. The "wild" horse migrated on its own initiative, having a much higher zoo-ecological intelligence, as well as being much more dynamic in character and having a stronger migratory inclination than the cow. And, as will be seen, the cow had to be recaptured and driven to that final destination by men on horseback.

From the earliest days of the *conquistadors,* nearly everywhere the Spanish intruders went, or tried to settle, the indigenous Indians were hostile. Whether it was a large traveling group such as the Coronado expedition, or attempts to establish tiny permanent settlements, the Indians were intent upon resisting and destroying the invaders. In many instances the fleet horses escaped. The Indians were smart enough to realize the advantages that the horses provided, although it was no easy matter for these primitive people, who had always done everything on foot, to pursue and capture such rapidly fleeing large creatures. Even when they did eventually capture the horse, it took time to learn how to retain and take advantage of these animals, which were entirely strange to them. The cattle were far more easily taken, but their characteristics were similar enough to the buffalo to prompt making immediate use of them for food.

The habitat into which the horses escaped was a natural one for their well-being, and they took readily to the free existence on the limitless grasslands, where for many centuries the buffalo had enjoyed ideal living conditions. Thus it was that the Spanish horse increased into large numbers of wild herds, which through the years spread northward across the entire expanse of plains and prairies. That spread was phenomenal. In all the annals of natural history in the world there is nothing regarding the introduction of a new species of large animal onto a continent that equals the spread of the horse on our western plains. Even today, the mulatto remnants of a few wild herds still struggle to survive. Many each year are captured and used by modern-day cowboys as rodeo bucking stock. Many more are run down by airplanes and shot to find a disgraceful end in tin cans sold for cat and dog food.

Some writers have disputed that the Coronado expedition had anything to do with the beginning of the wild-horse herds. This is of relatively small consequence. The indisputable fact is that the Spanish mustangs became residents in very large numbers over wide areas of our plains and prairies and that they were captured in large numbers, retamed, bred, and trained for special purposes by nearly every tribe of Indians in the West, in many instances before those Indians knew that Spaniards or Englishmen existed. It is also a well-established fact that acquisition of the horse provided the greatest cultural advancement for the western American Indians in all the hundreds of thousands of years of the development of their race. Literally overnight it converted the plains tribes from poor nomads on foot to prosperous warriors on horseback. And it was from these same wild herds, and from the Indian stock from the same origins, that the American cowboy acquired an early source of his riding mounts.

"Comanches Capturing Wild Horses"–GEORGE CATLIN (1834)–University Museum, Phila.

"Comanche Feats of Horsemanship"–GEORGE CATLIN (1834)–Smithsonian Institution

The herds of wild horses extended northward well beyond the area or knowledge of the early Spanish colonists in the Southwest. The earliest European visitors who traveled across the great plains to the Rocky Mountains, of what is today the United States, all report seeing herds of wild horses and finding that Indian tribes were in possession of the horses. It was not until George Catlin spent a number of years among these tribes that we had a comprehensive record, in both detailed description and on-the-spot pictures, of the "horse culture" and the broad scope of these people, when they were just emerging from the prehistoric era. Catlin lived among the Indians of both the northern and southern plains, and he was a particularly astute observer and recorder. He visited the nothern plains in 1832 and the southern plains in 1834.

George Catlin's trip into the deep Southwest in 1834 was with the historically important although almost disastrous military expedition of the 1st Regiment of Dragoons, sent out to explore the area and the possibilities of expanding the boundary of the United States into the region claimed by the Mexicans but dominated by the powerful and warlike Comanche Indians. This large tribe, spread along the border of Mexican Texas, was one of the least known of all the Plains Indians, although they were notorious for being defiantly hostile to both Mexicans and everyone else. As Catlin later recorded it: "The Comanches were enjoying the full bloom of their unspoiled primitive culture, and had already gained a wide reputation for their warlike skills as horsemen . . . and the finest riders on earth . . . capturing and subduing the finest of wild horses, and displaying the trickiest methods of riding." The Comanches were one of the first of the Indian tribes to capture the wild horses and to train these animals for their own use. The four hundred members of the U. S. 1st Regiment of Dragoons, a large number of whom were mounted on "eastern" horses, were received among the Comanches in a reserved and friendly manner. Catlin was afforded an excellent opportunity to observe close up these first horsemen of the plains.

Catlin described their wild horses as small but very powerful animals, generally about fourteen hands two to fifteen plus two in height (fifty-eight to sixty-two inches). "They graze over the vast plains . . . and congregate in large bands, oftimes to the amount of several hundreds together . . . the shyest animals of the prairies, detecting their enemy, Man, at a much greater distance than any other animal; and generally, when in motion, running several miles before they stop . . . and a band most pleasantly mottled; often presenting many varieties of colors and forms of marks. They are certainly animals capable of performing wonderful feats, and enduring great fatigue . . . subsisting entirely on the grass of the prairie. . . . Several times I had the opportunity of seeing the Indians pursue and take them with the lasso.

"The most frequent mode of catching the horse is by throwing the lasso from the back of a horse at full speed; and by choking the animal down. His lasso is a braided thong made of rawhide 15 to 20 yards in length, coiled upon his left arm, with a noose at the end; which he throws out to drop the coil over the horse's neck. This done, he holds back the other end or has it fastened to the girth of his own horse. He then dismounts, being dragged along by his strangling prize, until it falls from exhaustion. He then hurriedly fastens a pair of hobbles on its fore-feet, and a halter with a noose firmly around its jaw, before the lasso around the neck is relaxed enabling the horse to breathe; and leaning back on the thong with all his strength to prevent the horse from throwing itself too violently. This struggle generally lasts for about an hour, the Indian occasionally permitting the horse to get breath and regain its strength. Finally, when the animal is completely subdued, he gradually advances, hand over hand upon the tightened halter, to the horse's head, until the trembling and conquered animal allows the caressing hand of its new master to pat it on the nose; and in a few minutes to cover its eyes, when the exchange of a few deep-drawn breaths from their meeting nostrils seems to compromise the struggle; and the horse soon becomes the Indian's willing slave for the rest of its life."[13]

Among the most impressive feats of horsemanship practiced by the Comanches was their way of throwing themselves far down on the sides of their horses while riding at full speed in the heat of battle. "This is a stratagem learned and practiced by every young man in the tribe," wrote Catlin. "He is able to drop his body upon the side of the horse at the instant of passing an enemy, effectually screened from their weapons, as he lays in a horizontal position behind the body of his horse with his heel hanging over the horse's back, by which he has the power of throwing himself up again and changing to the other side if necessary. In this remarkable condition he will hang while at fullest speed, carrying with him his bow and shield, and also his lance of fourteen feet in length, all of which he can wield upon his enemy as he passes. . . . One day I coaxed a young fellow up close by offering him a few plugs of tobacco, and I found the explanation that a short hair halter was passed around under the neck of

"Sioux Buffalo Chase"–GEORGE CATLIN (1832)–American Heritage

the horse with both ends tightly braided into the mane on the withers, leaving a loop to hang under the neck. This made a sling into which the rider's elbow falls, taking the weight of his body on the middle of the upper arm. Into this loop the rider drops fearlessly, leaving his heel to hang over the horse's back to steady him and also to restore him when he wishes to regain his upright position. . . . I am ready without hesitation to pronounce the Comanches the most extraordinary horsemen I have seen and doubt very much whether any people in the world can surpass them." Other of the plains tribes learned to practice this, but nowhere with the perfection of the Comanche warriors. Some experts were able to shoot an arrow underneath the neck of their horse while it was going at full speed.

The Dragoons were fraught with illness throughout a large part of the journey; and when they finally returned to the starting point at Fort Gibson there were barely a hundred able-bodied men left to care for the ill survivors. Many were "litter cases," carried between two horses, including George Catlin, who along with many others was put in the garrison hospital. Thus ended the United States Government's first military expedition into the Southwest. About one-third of the men who started out gave up their lives, and a good many succumbed after they were brought back. Catlin never completely recovered. The difficulties were not caused by the Indians, but from being compelled to drink from stagnant pools, which were mud puddles made by wallowing buffalo.

From the land of the Comanches, Pawnees, and Apaches the herds of the wild

Spanish horses had spread northward over a broad sweep of the plains and high prairies. In 1832 George Catlin had previously visited and put on the record his pictures and text of most of the indigenous tribes of the northern plains: Sioux, Crow, Blackfoot, and their related and enemy groups, and everywhere he visited there was evidence of the wild horse herds and the horse culture these animals had occasioned among all those primitive people.

The prominent role played by the horse in the culture of the plains Indians began in early childhood. In raising a son properly, one tied him onto the back of a horse as soon as he could walk; and the most distinguished man of the tribe seldom could remember when he was not capable of riding. Horse stealing became an honorable pursuit; but this was always against tribes or groups outside their own, and they would go a long way and endure great risks to do so. The best way for a young man to get a fine wife was to steal enough horses to bribe her father; for older men, horses were the principal measurement of importance and wealth.

The buffalo had for centuries provided nearly all of the basic necessities of life for the plains Indians, and the horse had brought that primitive culture to almost complete fruition. The Indians had horses for all purposes. They had squaw horses for pulling travois to move camp, and buffalo horses and war horses. The Indians trained their horses well, for the Indians were highly intelligent in their own fields of necessity and survival. In some respects they were smarter than the white man. The buffalo-hunting horse was virtually a cowboy's "cutting horse," and as well or better trained; for a good buffalo horse could mean success or death to horse or rider. It was trained to approach the selected buffalo at a proper distance and position on

"A Crow Chief" — GEORGE CATLIN (1832)

"Horse Trader"–JOHN CLYMER

the right side of the quarry, in position for the Indian to make the most advantageous use of arrow or spear; and while the rider was using both hands for the use of his weapon, the well-trained horse was capable of swerving away at the instant an arrow or spear was thrust, to avoid a buffalo's natural reaction. Otherwise the horse could be impaled on the animal's horn, and if this happened there was the possibility the rider might be seriously injured or killed. It is highly probable that the cutting horse of the cowboy may have originated from the Indians' buffalo horse.

A chronology of the spread of the Spanish horse northward may always be little more than conjecture. The Lewis and Clark expedition across the northern part of the present United States provides a substantial record for the years 1804–5. This was strictly an investigative undertaking, and the records are clear. They were not the earliest visitors in the regions they traversed, although their primary objective was to report on everything they observed. When the expedition arrived at the Mandan Village, near the present Montana-North Dakota boundary, to spend the first winter, they found those Indians in possession of a plentiful number of horses that had originated from the early Spanish stock. They also found a Scotch trader who had come down from Canada to barter with the Mandans for horses and buffalo robes to take back with him. That trader's name happened to be Hugh McCracken, an ancestor of mine. Far more important, however, is the fact that the Mandans in 1804 had horses to trade and be taken farther north; and that the Lewis and Clark expedition found horses possessed by practically every Indian tribe they encountered all the way

"Vaqueros"–W. H. D. KOERNER

across the continent. One entry in their journals is particularly significant: "Captain Meriweather Lewis, under date of August 14, 1805, records that he saw Indian horses, some of which had Spanish brands, and one of these a Spanish bit. This was near the Shoshone River."[14]

Descended as all of these horses presumably were from the hot-blooded stock of the Spanish *conquistadors* and the domesticated training their ancestors had, it is only natural that when these animals reverted to an unrestrained primeval state this would accentuate their fiery characteristics. After a few generations of this complete freedom and depending on their self-preservation, they may have lost some of their classic parade style, although they gained a great deal in strength and stamina, and all their senses developed infinitely sharper. By the time they were acquired by our American cowboy, they had become a cavalier's mount of unexcelled qualities.

Chapter 7

TEXAS LONGHORN BONANZA

The Spanish longhorn cattle came to the northern plains much later than the horse. They had to be driven, and were slow-moving as well as difficult to manage on the trail, particularly in small numbers. Old, well-subdued oxen made strong and economical beasts for hauling heavily loaded wagons, although trails across mountains and wild country were no place for a wagon of any kind. Even their value as food was not sufficient to justify the inconvenience, for in those early days there was almost everywhere a more than sufficient supply of wild game of one kind or another. Interestingly enough, however, some of the mixed-blood progeny of this original Spanish longhorn stock reached the northern plains by a long, circuitous route via Oregon, and contributed to the important transition from longhorn to shorthorn stock.

For more than half a century control of the Oregon region was strongly contested by the fur companies as well as the federal governments of Canada and the United States. Spanish ships had explored the coast a long time before, although it was not until 1792 that Captain Robert Gray was the first of record to sail into the Great River of the West and name it after his ship *Columbia*. Then the Lewis and Clark expedition of 1804–5 brought widespread attention and interest to the verdant valleys and mild climate, as well as the richly abundant fur of the Oregon region. John McLaughlen, the chief factor of the Hudson's Bay Fur Company at Fort Vancouver, was an empire builder as well as a collector of furs, and he strongly encouraged the coming of permanent settlers, and welcomed all of any national origin. And here again religious missionaries played an important role in the settlement and development of a wilderness country. Among these were Jason and Daniel Lee, Methodists (1834); Samuel Parker (1835); and the following year Marcus Whitman and Harry H. Spaulding, Presbyterians. The latter were accompanied by their wives, who were the first women of record to travel overland and pioneer the soon to become historically famous Oregon Trail. Previously the transportation and immigration to the Pacific Coast country from the still-infant United States and northern European countries had been by sailing ships "around the Horn."

Some cattle had been brought to Oregon by sea, although these were of the mild-natured shorthorn varieties, or "American cattle," as they became known, in contrast to the Spanish longhorns. Factor McLaughlen had a few cattle at Fort Vancouver, but as families and babies became an increasing part of the Oregon frontier life, the desire and necessity for more cattle developed; and the nearest supply in plenty was the Spanish region of California. This led to the first overland trail drive of Spanish longhorns by Americans, and one might say the first American cowboys.[15] It was apparently a joint project instigated by Philip Legat Edwards (a Kentuckian) and John McLaughlen, the Canadian Hudson's Bay Fur Company factor. Thus the Willamette Cattle Company was organized on January 14, 1837. Ewing Young from Tennessee, who had previously trapped in New Mexico and California, was elected leader; Edwards was named treasurer, to negotiate the purchase of the cattle; and William A. Slocum acted as agent for the United States Government and contributed purchase funds as well as the cost of transporting the party by ship to California. The purpose of the undertaking was to supply the farmer-settlers in the Oregon country with cattle, so necessary to the conquering of the wilderness.

The expedition left Campment du Sable on January 17, 1837, and after many vicissitudes and delays by small sailing crafts finally arrived at Yerba Buena, the Bay of San Francisco, on March 1. After many further difficulties in making arrangements to obtain the cattle, they began the even more difficult and hazardous task of making the overland cattle trail drive back to Oregon. Of the 729 head of stock with which the drive started, 630 were to reach Oregon. This contribution from the Mexican Californians, which helped the Oregon settlers, was later repaid by Oregonians who traveled south to assist in making California a new part of the territory of the United States.

"The Texas Longhorn" (PHOTOGRAPH)

The Edwards diary gives a running account of the many arduous and dangerous difficulties encountered in driving the irascible longhorns on their journey to Oregon. The diary ends abruptly with the entry for September 18, describing harassment and an attack by a group of hostile Indians, who made an attempt to ambush both men and cattle. From other sources, however, it has been established that Edwards and Young successfully reached their destination with the 630 cattle in the middle of October.

Oregon and the Oregon Trail became enchanting bywords in the thoughts of many adventure-minded Yankees whose families had settled in Kentucky, Missouri, Ohio, and elsewhere in the Midwest; and a good many of these made the long trek across the Great Plains, considerably before the Gold Rush to California began. Most of these pioneer families had cattle and horses whose ancestors had been brought across the Atlantic from countries of northern Europe. Succeeding generations of highly domesticated stock moved with the western migration of the English, who had originally settled Tidewater Virginia, and with the Swedes along Chesapeake Bay; the Germans in Pennsylvania; the Dutch in the Hudson Valley; and the French, Scotch, and English in New England and Nova Scotia. The cattle that these home-seeking immigrants brought with them were principally Devon, Hereford, Jersey, and shorthorn; and their horses were sturdier varieties than those of the Spanish. The cattle were not in large numbers, and were strictly barnyard stock. The "American cattle" served well to pull the westward-bound covered wagons conveying women and children and household necessities. The animals served later in plowing fields and supplying milk and butter, and their meat was far superior to that of the bony, half-wild

"In His Texas Habitat" (PHOTOGRAPH)

"Rounding Up Strays"–EDWARD BOREIN

Spanish longhorns. Across the plains over the Oregon Trail the caravans plodded, slowly and methodically, not stopping on the arid way until they reached the green valleys of the far Northwest. Strangely enough, an unsuspected destiny was to dictate the time when the offspring of these undramatic breeds of barnyard shorthorn cattle would supersede the vast herds of Spanish longhorns in the development of the great cattle industry on our western plains. And, in like manner, the less fiery horses of the immigrants from the East would prove to have a far-reaching influence on the character of the cowboys' riding stock. Furthermore, the famed Oregon Trail would see the progeny of those same immigrant cattle and horses traveling in a reverse migration back to Wyoming, Montana, and adjacent states, to contribute in large degree to a great transition in the development of both cattle and horses.

In the meantime, cattle history had been in the making in Texas since the end of the seventeenth century. Settlement from Mexico was begun in 1690, and several ecclesiastical missions, military *presidios,* and civil headquarters were soon established. A considerable number of longhorn cattle were driven into the region, along with other varieties of stock in a program to begin the conversion of the wilderness. From the beginning, however, there was a plague of political struggles, rebellions, and wars, from within and outside, as well as almost constant harassment by hostile Indians. On two occasions the French from nearby Louisiana tried to establish settlements in Spanish America, and were driven out. As early as 1824 there were a considerable number of adventurous colonists from the United States who tried to gain a foothold in the region, and they too were driven out. But other Americans came, and in 1830 an official decree was issued forbidding any immigrants from the United States from entering as colonists. This situation persisted until the Republic of Texas was admitted to the Union as a state on December 29, 1845.

Through it all the missions and their Indian converts, as well as the Spanish-speaking immigrants from Mexico, and the smattering of Americans, depended on the bony longhorn cattle as a source of food, as well as hides for leather and tallow for candles. The longhorns became an easy means of subsistence. They ran free. When anyone needed beef or leather or tallow, all they had to do was go out and kill one. The little bands propagated into large herds. Many of the cattle wandered away, and they became increasingly wild. But there were always plenty to be found, and they became so numerous and of such small value that all a Mexican had to do was ride out and take what was desired. So why should one bother to waste time and effort, to try to control what took care of itself? And anyhow, it was much more pleasurable to dress in one's best and go with some friends to a fiesta—or just sit in the shade and think of nothing at all.

The longhorn cattle were apparently as much inclined to indulge in the indolent life as any of the Mexicans. During the heat of the day they stood lazily in the inadequate shade of the chaparral thickets, and in the evening they wandered out to feed. For them, it was also an easy life; and they multiplied like compound interest. In appearance the longhorn was impressive; but it was far from a handsome beast.

"An Unfriendly Longhorn"–FREDERIC REMINGTON

For a bovine he seemed to be all legs, head, and horns, with bony knobs protruding around his prominent knees, hips, and along the backbone, giving the critter an ungainly look. In his broad, square face were a deep-set pair of large, onion-shaped eyes that always had an evil look; and surmounting all was the pair of widely spreading horns that in extraordinary specimens went nearly nine feet from tip to tip. The tight, leathery skin that draped his unshapely body only added an impression of half-starved wildness, and he had a temper that was a classic for stubborn and pugnacious insociability. He seemed to have a particular hatred for men. Theodore Roosevelt once made the remark that a "mean Texas longhorn could be the most dangerous wild animal in America."

Prosperity for the longhorn meant half-edible grass, an occasional spiny mesquite tree with some pods left on the branches, and water that did not have to be fit for a human to drink. Wherever there was water, of one kind or another, the longhorns were to be found not too far away; and it was to the most convenient of these places that the meat and hide hunters went to find them. Most of the meat was left to rot.

As the little settlements around the *presidios* grew larger, and the converted Indians around the missions developed a taste for civilized ways, the demand for leather and candles increased; and some of the more progressive of the Mexicans

"The Land of Missions"–FREDERIC REMINGTON

began spending more time at the crude business of hunting longhorns for their hides and tallow. This, apparently, became the origin of the common designation "Mexican greasers." Some of the more ambitious of the hide and tallow hunters took a more businesslike attitude and began peddling hides or tanned leather and tallow to communities outside their own. Some even built living places out in the areas near the important sources of water that attracted concentrations of the longhorns. As the business increased, some took their families, and the locations became more permanently established as crude little ranches. Then problems arose in defending themselves against attacks by hostile Indians, as well as in upholding their squatters' rights to the locations. This could be considered the beginning of ranch life on the western plains. The rights to the grass and the water were considered free to those who got there first and were able to defend them against all intruders. This set the pattern for the unwritten law of the land, which was followed and adhered to throughout the open range country, and it persisted throughout the era of the old-time cattle-raising industry.

The traffic in hides and tallow prospered; and it wasn't long until these products were being hauled to points on the Gulf of Mexico, to be taken from there by boats to New Orleans and other centers of population. This led to more and more squatter

"Going to the Fiesta"–EDWARD BOREIN

"Warning of an Attack"–FREDERIC REMINGTON

ranches being established at advantageous locations farther away from the *presidios*. Some adventurous Americans, who were determined to stay in the country, married Mexican or Spanish women, and went into the new cattle business on the free land, where free water and free longhorns were available. Some of these outposts in the wilderness, especially those located in particularly good locations, became the objects of attack by hide hunters who were perfectly willing to kill off a few neighbor *rancheros* or outsiders in order to establish themselves in the location. Sometimes newcomers set up headquarters so close by that one or the other had to fight for survival. These incidents may be considered the beginning of the range wars on the plains that sometimes involved large numbers of contestants and became bloody affairs.

Through the natural processes of nature the wild longhorns increased to a remarkable extent and spread over such a wide area that the activities of the hide hunters made but little effect upon the total number of cattle in the broad expanse of Texas. Thus the big bonanza in longhorns developed of its own accord, the impact of which was to become of great importance to the whole cattle industry on our western plains as well as to the development and economy of the United States.

"Lassoing a Grizzly (in California)" –JAMES WALKER

"The Talley" —CHARLIE DYE

Chapter 8

LONGHORNS IN A THOUSAND THICKETS

The lamentable Civil War had an ironic although important influence in the development of the cattle industry, which became a significant factor in generating the settlement and general economy of the American West. The war inflicted deep wounds of sorrow, widespread, slow-healing bitterness, as well as a blight of adversity upon stay-at-homes that affected survivors in the North as well as the South. This aftermath of human misfortune was particularly true in the spacious regions of western Texas, where a sparce population of hardy American pioneers had been caught at a time when they were struggling to establish a livable existence and management of the unfriendly natural resources of the areas in which they hoped their future family generations would continue to make their homes.

By the time Texas became a part of the United States, long before the Civil War, there had been a slow but steady influx of adventurous Americans from Kentucky, Missouri, and Georgia, as well as from the New England states and elsewhere. A good many of these pioneers were single men who married Mexicans, although there were men with families as well. For the most part the newcomers provided an element that was considerably more progressive than the original Spanish-Mexican inhabitants. Many of the newcomers decided there was a promising future in cattle ranching. There was an abundance of grasslands that could be taken by squatter's rights, or leased or purchased at extremely low cost, or occupied on a profit-sharing arrangement with the big Spanish Colonial land-grant owners. And there was the vast abundance of half-wild unbranded longhorns, as well as the herds of wild horses, with which those pioneers with ambition and courage might establish themselves on a working ranch with promising hopes for the future. From those who went into this field with real determination developed a particularly rugged breed of rural individual. From the Mexican *vaqueros* they adopted all the gear and methods of riding and handling the mean and obstreperous longhorns; and many of them became as expert or better *vaqueros* than the best of the *vaqueros* themselves. By the time the Civil War became a reality, a considerable number of the Americans were pretty well on their way toward establishing themselves in the cattle industry, although in a rather crude manner and with but small benefit of profit.

Texas and Texans naturally became a part of the Confederacy. Virtually all of the hard-riding American *rancheros* became a strong bulwark of the Confederate cavalry. The Southern Army took about every able-bodied man except those too old or too young to be acceptable for the extremes of warfare. It was under these extenuating circumstances that the youngsters who were left behind had to assume the duties of riding herd on the family's longhorns; and thus these youngsters earned for themselves the original designation of "cow boys".

The war virtually put to an end what little marketing there had been in Texas cattle; and even on the ranches that had become modestly operative, many of the longhorns that had come under control were allowed to wander off and return to the wild herds.

During the early stages of the war there were efforts made to drive cattle through to the Confederate troops beyond the Mississippi; and this was even continued to a lesser extent after the Union forces had captured New Orleans in 1862, and effected a blockade of the big river as well as the Gulf ports and overland routes. However, running the risks of confiscation of the cattle and being killed by the patrols, some Texan cattle were ferried and even swam across the Mississippi during the darkness of night, and then driven to Confederate camps as far as Mobile, Alabama. But as the war continued, the marketing of the longhorns for even much-needed beef or hides continued to diminish and then literally died. The value of a prime animal became as low as two dollars, and buyers were difficult to find. As a result, the long-

"Trail Boss"—EDWARD BOREIN

"Rounding Up a Stray"–EDWARD BOREIN

horns were left to roam at will again, with but little molestation except by an occasional meat hunter. In addition to the leather and tallow from the leggy members of the half-wild herds, it had been learned that their hoofs were salable for glue and the horns for the making of fancy "Spanish" combs, although the total amount of remuneration to be gained was no great incentive to induce any large number of hunters into the field. Thus the longhorns continued to increase prodigiously. Historian Hubert Howe Bancroft gives confirmation of this in his two-volume work, *North Mexican States and Texas*[16]: "In Texas the cattle increased from a few score of thousand in the 1820's to an estimated 4,000,000 in 1860 — making a 10 to 1 majority of *Bos taurus* over *Homo sapiens.*" During the war period that ratio was greatly increased.

When the Confederate soldiers returned to their homes in the late spring and early summer of 1865, they found desolation upon the whole land. This was particularly true in the rural areas. Even the Confederate money they had earned and saved, and received as mustering-out pay, was virtually worthless. A good many of the able-bodied men who had gone to war did not return. Most of the small and large herds had disappeared into the badlands. Nor was there any incentive to round up the stock, for there was no local market where the cattle could be sold. For most Texans obtaining meat for the table was only a matter of going out and shooting a wild longhorn.

The economy of the region was in a desperate state. So was the morale. Fresh in the minds of everyone was the historically embarrassing occasion of April 9, 1865, at Appomattox Court House, Virginia, when General Lee surrendered to General

Grant; followed on April 26 at Durham Station, North Carolina, when Johnston surrendered to Sherman. The war had cost the lives of a lot of good men, and there was deep and understandable bitterness on both sides, although it was naturally stronger among those who had lost the conflict. There were a lot of empty saddles in the back country of western Texas, where those who had been too young to go to war were left pretty much alone to carry on by whatever manner or means they might be able to devise.

The longhorn cattle offered an inexhaustible harvest that was spread throughout the land and was literally free to everyone for the taking. But it seemed not worth the taking. There was no local market, and previous experience in finding a distant market had proven to be not worth the difficulties and the results to be gained. According to the *Agriculture Report of the Tenth United States Census of* 1880, a few small herds were rounded up and driven on-the-hoof to New Orleans "previous to the Mexican revolt against Spain in 1821" (p. 965). And by 1842 small herds were being driven to Galveston and Shreveport, Louisiana, to be transported by boat to New Orleans. But because of the economic situation throughout the entire South following the war any such similar undertaking was not worthy of serious consideration. The abundance of longhorns seemed to be destined to be little more than a poor man's source of free meat to feed his hungry family.

Up North a different series of circumstances had been developing following the end of the Civil War. The California gold rush, with its aura of easily obtained wealth and high adventure in the American West, had become an alluring fascination among young and old in nearly every American home, as well as many in Europe. The overland trails had become well trodden from the Mississippi westward across the great plains, and California as well as Oregon had gained a considerable added population by many ships sailed around the southern end of South America. A good many of the California-bound covered-wagon families had stopped along the way to establish themselves in fertile areas, and this had led to further attraction to the West. Conscious of the many possibilities that were offered in the unsettled and undeveloped regions between the Mississippi and the Rocky Mountains, one of the greatest human migrations in history was begun.

To keep pace with the increasing movement of families out across the great plains, as well as to provide a substantial transportation between the eastern area of the country and the important developments of the Pacific regions, railroads were being built westward where the overland trails were, but a short time before, the only routes of slow-plodding travel. Along the steel rails the beginnings of towns were springing up, and around these a constant influx of settlers were plowing the land. Professional hunters were busy killing buffalo to supply meat for the thousands of hungry laborers who were building the railroads, and buffalo meat was a common staple in the newly built places where food and supplies could be obtained. But the buffalo were not to be had at all times, and the supply was generally insufficient. It was becoming obvious that the time would come when there would be no more buffalo; and the need for a dependable source of beef to accommodate the rapidly increasing demand became of major importance.

The only supply of meat that might become available as a constant source and in sufficient quantity was the vast number of longhorn cattle that was known to exist in Texas. Thus a situation developed in which the people of two parts of the United States so recently engaged on opposing sides of a very bloody Civil War found themselves in the rather ironic circumstances of being parties to very critical matters of supply and demand by which they might be of important benefit to each other.

There was but one way to get the longhorns to a market in the North. That was to round up herds of the half-wild creatures and drive them there on the hoof. No one knew better than the back-country Texans just how difficult and risky that was going to be. It would not be any simple matter to capture and control a few hundred wild and unwilling longhorns; and to trail drive them northward through a thousand miles of rough and unfamiliar country occupied by very hostile Indians would be a desperate if not impossible proposition.

Few of the wild-eyed long-horned mavericks had ever felt a rawhide lasso around their neck. To flush them out of thorny thickets was as difficult as trying to secure a noose on any part of their anatomy. Riding in on a horse was as bad as going in on foot. Some of the bovine belligerents were just mean enough to lie in ambush waiting to charge a rider on horseback, and there weren't many horses in Texas that could escape disaster under those close-quarter circumstances; for, in spite of a six-foot spread of horns, the big bulls could bust through the worst thickets and thorns in a most surprising manner. Or if met face to face in an open space, a big old mossback might just stand and snort defiance, then suddenly charge like a mad rhinoceros. It was easy enough to

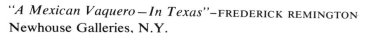

"A Mexican Vaquero — In Texas" – FREDERICK REMINGTON
Newhouse Galleries, N.Y.

shoot them down for hides or meat, but capturing and driving them in large numbers was quite a different matter.

It was generally easier to round up the wily beasts when they came out of the thickets on moonlit nights to feed or drink. Then the mounted riders could race to cut off their retreat, lasso and throw the leaders, hogtie all four feet, and leave them to thrash and bellow until they were exhausted. Many were left overnight and into the next day, when their legs were so lame that when finally released they were hardly able to get to their feet and keep from falling down again. It was a more drastic way than "busting" a mean wild horse and teaching him he wasn't his own boss anymore. The meanest of the longhorns might thrash about so violently they would break a leg and have to be shot, and left to furnish meals for the coyotes and buzzards. Not every longhorn had to be broken that way, although there were generally a few bad ones in every large bunch. If the top bosses could be gotten under control, the others were usually inclined to follow the leader. Like wild animals that travel in herds or packs, such as deer, elk, and buffalo, as well as wolves, there is respect and dependence on the old and wiser ones, whom the younger members will follow.

It was common practice to use trained oxen, known as *cabestros,* to aid in the roundups. The training of such oxen was as old as bull fighting in Spain. Some *vaqueros* carried a drill of fine steel, with which to bore a hole through the horn of a wild longhorn, into which to insert a steel pin to aid in fastening the obstinate wild one to the horn of a *cabestro.* Thus lashed horn-to-horn by means of a strong rawhide thong, the newly captured bovine could be forced to travel in the desired direction. They were lashed closely horn-to-horn to prevent the wild one from goring the trained ox.

Under the most favorable of circumstances, it took men with a great amount of guts, stamina, and disregard for personal danger to round up a bunch of Texas longhorns, hold them together, and drive them in a desired direction. After getting them out in the open and in some semblance of being herded, the task was really only begun. To keep them bunched and moving away from the wild haunts where they had been born and grew up often called for the most strenuous efforts on the part of every rider as well as the horse he rode. There was invariably a bolter, and when he took off he had to be quickly stopped, or the whole herd would follow. The quicker and harder he was "tailed" or "busted" with a lasso, the less chance there was for more trouble. Sometimes the treatment had to be applied more than once, until the surprised and bruised recalcitrant bovine struggled to his feet and decided it was better for him to go along with the rest. Men who could follow this strenuous routine day after day were men who indeed could sit tall in the saddle.

Rounding up the longhorns was only the beginning. The animals would then have to be assembled under a controlled situation until there were enough to make such a long drive worth while. There was also the problem of enlisting capable men willing to make such a trip, especially since there were serious doubts as to what sort of reception any Texan might receive up in Yankeeland. Furthermore, in addition to all the misgivings, there was the question as to whether the bony, almost worthless longhorns could be sold for enough to justify the undertaking. And the prospect that Indians might ambush and annihilate all the men in order to capture the cattle was not a pleasant thought. In fact, a good many of the initial trail drivers and their longhorns failed to make it through to a desired destination. To organize and undertake those first trail drives for an indefinite marketplace in the North took an extraordinary amount of fortitude and courage on the part of all concerned.

However, the need for cattle in the North was a real one. Beef of any kind was a major necessity to feed the thousands of hard-working laborers engaged in building the railroads. Many of those who had joined the migration to become permanent settlers on the land, or to set up shop in the new towns to pursue a trade, brought cattle with them, although these were "eastern" shorthorn stock, and there were more important uses for these animals than slaughtering them for table food. They were used to haul the homesteaders' covered wagons, later to supply family milk and in many instances they were used for pulling the plows to turn over the virgin prairie grass for planting first crops. There was not an adequate supply of draft oxen more suitable for the more laborious duty. The Army also needed beef to feed the increasing number of soldiers who were being sent out as protection against hostile Indians. Furthermore, the prices being paid for cattle of any kind were many times more than the most generous asking price for longhorns in Texas. The only problem was to get those cattle driven across the eight hundred to a thousand miles of dangerous wilderness that separated the source of supply from the waiting markets.

"Two Pike County Arrivals"–FREDERIC REMINGTON

"The Mexican Type"–FREDERIC REMINGTON

In the summer of 1866 a few herds of the half-wild Texas longhorns were gathered together by adventurous "drovers," who with the aid of a minimum of inexperienced cowboys got their cattle headed northeasterly in the general direction of St. Louis. Nearly all of these initial drives met with disaster. The long lines of easily spooked bovines were like sitting ducks for the bands of hostile Indians, who had little difficulty in stampeding the cattle to kill what they wanted; and lucky were the cowboys who escaped with their lives.

One of the first of these early drives was led by a very enterprising nineteen-year-old Texan by the name of James M. Dougherty. With a well-picked small group of cowboys, he got together a herd of about a thousand longhorns and crossed the Red River near Rock Bluffs on the northern border of Texas, determined to get his cattle to the market in St. Louis. Getting through the worst of the Indian country, they finally relaxed when they entered the state of Missouri, feeling that ultimate success was almost won. However, after successfully contending with the hazards of Indians, swimming rivers, and surviving stampedes and other dangers and difficulties, they were suddenly entrapped by what appeared to be a completely disastrous experience.

In the sparsely settled areas of southern Kansas and Missouri there were gangs of bushwhacking white hillbillies who quickly assembled to assume the role of hoodlum brigands and prey on herds of longhorn cattle being brought north from Texas. Whether or not these early-day back woods settlers realized or cared whether the Civil War was over would probably not have influenced them, for it was a continuation of border warfare, by a people who needed no excuse for depredations that could be beneficial to themselves; and young Dougherty, together with his cowboys and all his cattle, unfortunately fell into the virtual captivity of one of these bands of plunderers.

The highly regarded contemporary historian Joseph G. McCoy, in his 1874 book *Historic Sketches of the Cattle Trade of the West and Southwest,*[17] records the account of Dougherty and his misadventures. He referred to these groups of border brigands, such as the gang that ambushed and captured Dougherty and his entire trail outfit, as "determined, organized, armed mobs, more lawless, insolent and imperious than bands of wild savages . . . outlaws and thieves, glad of an excuse to pillage, kill and steal. . . . The practice was to go in force and armed to the teeth, surround the drover, insult him by words such as only a cowardly bully knows how to use; spit in his face, snatch handsful of beard out of his face, tie him to a tree and whip him with anything they could lay their hands on; tie a rope around his neck and choke him. In short, provoke him to a demonstration of resistance and self defense, then kill him and straightaway proceed to appropriate his herd. It was an idle waste of time to talk about protection of the law, for such a thing was utterly impossible." (p. 21)

McCoy relates the story of the Dougherty incident as a case history of the banditry being practiced by these preying gangs of hillbillies in southern Kansas and Missouri, describing how the Texans and their longhorns were captured by the rough and heavily armed characters "dressed in the coarsest tow [fiber yarn], homemade hide shoes, all surmounted by a coonskin cap of great antiquity and unmistakably home manufacture . . . and visages bearing witness of the lowest order of humanity."

Young Dougherty tried to reason with the members of the mob. But this was "like preaching morality to an alligator. . . . Then they dragged him from his saddle, disarmed him, tied him fast to a tree with his own picket rope, then proceeded to whip him with hickory withes [branches] in the most brutal manner."

The herd of longhorns was stampeded, while several of the Missourians took turns in beating their bound victim, as if taking sadistic pleasure to thus kill him. Far more familiar with handling spooked Texas longhorns than were the outlaws who had been assigned that task, Dougherty's cowboys gained control of the madly rushing thousand head of cattle, and by almost a miracle they managed to keep them following their leaders and thundering on until the less hardy horses of the would-be cattle thieves were unable to continue any farther and were left far behind.

Half dead, Dougherty was eventually untied and ordered to ride out of the country, in the opposite direction from which the cattle had gone. Stripped of everything on his person that was worth taking, he was barely able to get up into the saddle, and minus his six-shooter, the young drover was glad to be able to ride slowly away, leaving his assailants no doubt believing that the herd of cattle was safe in the control of their compatriots.

After riding a mile or more in a half stupor, one of the young drover's men, who had risked staying behind to be of whatever assistance might be possible, rode out of the underbrush and overtook him; and the two circled to pick up the tracks of the stampeding longhorns. Eventually they overtook and joined the others, with the herd under complete control. Keeping on at a forced pace, they headed for the northeast corner of the Indian Territory. Not until they were a safe distance away from the near tragedy was the herd stopped for Dougherty to recover from his ordeal. Then they pushed on to Fort Scott, Kansas, where the cattle were sold for a very satisfactory profit.

Dougherty returned to Texas, and promptly sat about getting together another trail herd to take north. This became his permanent occupation, taking from one thousand to four thousand head on each trip to Kansas. By 1874, when the McCoy book was published, Dougherty had acquired a large fine cattle ranch in Colorado, and was taking a position "among the best and most substantial citizens of the great new West." His first experience was enough to deter himself as well as others from attempting further trail drives from Texas; but it certainly did not.

The demand for cheap beef in the northern territories was great. Railroad construction work was spreading out into most regions of the new West, and the appetites of the thousands of laborers could be satisfied with most any meat that was chewable. Texas longhorns were by no means the choicest of table beef, but they were cheap and perfectly satisfactory to the markets. There were commissary agents ready to buy whole herds upon delivery on-the-hoof. There was also a growing demand on the part of individuals and small groups of enterprising pioneers who were interested in buying hardy Texas cattle to establish their own herds on the free grass of the open range that spread over millions of square miles of the northern plains. The market was there, waiting for the Texans to bring their longhorns up the trails.

"The Cattle Drive"–JOHN CLYMER–Whitney Gallery, Cody, Wyo.

Chapter 9

MEN TO MATCH
THE LONGHORNS

After the first small drives got through, it became evident that the profits were worth the gamble, although the right kind of men to do the job were hard to find. Those with experience were almost nonexistent. A lot of physical endurance and guts were fundamental, although being a good horseman, roper, and having know-how in handling longhorns were also essential. In addition, it was necessary to know how to use a gun and keep your cool when a bunch of screeching wild Indians came dashing out of nowhere in *kamikaze* fashion. Sometimes a working day literally meant twenty-four hours in the saddle, or more; the food was meager; and the pay, only about a dollar a day. There were Mexican *vaqueros* who were excellent riders and ropers and knew the half-wild longhorns like they knew the allurement of a pretty *señorita*. They also had plenty of guts. But the long, interminable grind of trail-driving a big, slow-moving herd from southern Texas across hundreds of miles of wilderness infested with hostile savages was not for the Mexican *vaquero*. He liked too much to mix his work with a bit of fiesta, or just to sit in the shade and snooze. An American, even with a lot to learn about the essentials and necessities, was far preferable; but these were not easy to find.

The most desirable of all were the young American "cow boys" who had been forced into the handling of cattle when their brothers or fathers had gone away to war. A good many of these became the early drovers and taught others whom they induced to go along. Some of these, who survived several successful trail drives, became wealthy men; and some eventually became prominent figures in the cattle-raising industry on the northern plains.

The pattern for the early trail drives was a simple and natural one, and it was not substantially changed during the relatively short period of overland on-the-hoof delivery of longhorns from Texas to the northern markets. Although the cattle were normally rather slow-traveling animals, they were kept moving along as briskly as possible, so that when the time came to stop for the night they would be tired and more inclined to feed and bed down, and give less trouble. According to McCoy, "with each

herd are about two men to every three hundred head of cattle."[18] This would seem
hardly enough, even when the herd was moving along peacefully, without the usual
difficulties that faced every trip. With one or two good lead oxen, it took a cowboy
on each side to insure keeping the long line of animals moving in the desired direction;
and it was the leaders that set the pace. Other cowboys were required to ride alongside
the main column, to keep strays or "bolters" from breaking away and possibly causing
a large group to follow. Still others were needed to bring up the rear and keep the lag-
gers up tight, as well as to look after the extra horses. A herd of a thousand cattle
might string out for a mile or more under normal traveling conditions. This made the
herd very vulnerable to the hazards of the trail. Trouble was always imminent and
could prove disastrous unless the cowboys were able to quickly gain control of the
situation.

Crossing the numerous river barriers on the trail was a major concern to the trail
herders. Good lead oxen were as a rule easily induced to go into the water, even when
swimming was necessary; and the rest usually followed to the opposite bank. However, it was not so easy when the large rivers were swollen by fast-moving spring
floods of boiling muddy water. On these occasions the cowboys had to work fast to
get the cattle into the water so as to avoid the animals bunching up in large numbers
and breaking off in one direction or another. A cowboy might have to put a lasso onto
the lead ox and plunge his horse into the water to swim ahead to induce the herd to
follow along after them. More serious were the times when a large group of the
swimming herd would for some unknown reason begin floundering around in a circle
of frantic confusion. On these occasions the cowboy would have to break up the
panic and get the cattle moving toward the opposite bank or they could drown each
other.

Sometimes it was necessary for the cowboy to swim his horse right in among the
floundering, struggling mass of longhorns. This was always at the risk of being knocked

"Trailing Cattle North"–FREDERIC REMINGTON

out of the saddle and being compelled to swim for his life. If this happened and he was fortunate enough to grab hold of the tail of a steer or his horse, the cowboy could hope to be hauled to where he could make it to safety under his own power. But there were times when he was not so fortunate. Probably more cowboys lost their lives in situations such as this than from any other cause during the trail drives. It was a dangerous time for the cattle also. When the flood waters were running full and swift, it often swept the herd downstream, scattering them for considerable distances along both riverbanks. It took extra-hard work to round them up again and start them in the right direction. And there were generally losses from drowning or escaping.

The most feared incident of all was a stampede during the night. When the night was inky dark and the lightning flashed zigzag streaks across the black dome of the heavens, the cowboy's skill and courage were put to their greatest test. When the thunder jarred the earth and electric balls of fire split the wind-lashed sheets of rain, a nervous herd of easily spooked longhorns was most apt to suddenly explode and go thundering away in any direction. It happened on a good many occasions, and it could be that the frequently used term "the thundering herd" originated from these occasions. But to the cowboys who were there at the moment and had to do something to stop it, it was "hell in the night." Nor was it necessary to have thunder and lightning to start a great herd on one of these wild night stampedes. It could be as little a thing as the horse of a night herder stepping on a brittle stick, or relieving his boredom with a rattling snort, or the sharp sneeze of the night herder himself. The most minor incident could, as if by magic, ignite the stampede of a thousand cattle.

When a stampede started, the cowboy had to ride blindly at full speed to get alongside the leaders, not to stop them, for that was impossible, but to turn them either to the right or to the left, gradually leading their course into a large circle, the circumference of which the cowboy would attempt to narrow down as rapidly as possible. The object of this would be to eventually bring the herd together, so the cattle were

"Mobbing Texas Trail Driver in South Missouri" (c. 1866)

rushing about in as small an area as possible, and eventually become too tired to run any farther. Then the cowboy would begin to sing his favorite midnight lullaby in a voice as loud as he could manage, hoping that this magic communication between man and beast might add to the calming of the herd. Strangely enough, it often did.

Otherwise, several unfortunate things were apt to happen in which the cowboy had his own hide to worry about, as well as controlling the herd. Plunging blindly through the darkness in pursuit of the "thundering herd," his horse was apt to stumble and fall to the ground. In such instances, and they did occur, both horse and rider could be cut to pieces by the sharp hoofs of a hundred or more plunging longhorns. The whole herd might continue the mad run for as much as twenty miles or more before stopping. Stragglers might be scattered along the way, to wander into thickets to be lost from the others; or the herd might break up into numerous groups that would branch off in half a dozen different directions. To round up all of a widely scattered herd could take a lot of time, or even be impossible. There was also the possibility that a stampeding herd in the darkness of night might suddenly come to a deep cut-bank or sharply defined ravine and go plunging over to pile up in a struggling mass of injured or dead cattle. There was always the chance that a cowboy and his horse might be right in the midst of this, or be buried underneath.

Those early trail drives of Texas longhorns served as the hard and uncompromising molding ground for the American cowboy of the future. It was on these trips that the evolution of the cowboy began and the American way of handling large herds of range cattle was developed. The cowboys were a raggedy lot, embarked upon one of the toughest jobs any man on earth could undertake. Among those early trail drivers were some Confederate ex-soldiers, who had lost about everything but life itself, and did not care very much what happened to them in the future. There was also an occasional English problem son "remittance man" who had been paid to stay away from

"A Midnight Stampede of Longhorns" (c. 1868)

"The Trail Herd"–EDWARD BOREIN

home, and other ne'er-do-wells who joined up for the sheer adventure that might come on the trip; and there were individuals who just wanted to get out of Texas, for reasons that were strictly personal and not to be divulged. They were a mixed group, of varied backgrounds, but by the time the herd had crossed the Red River, the sharing of daily hardships, of midnight stampedes, of attacks by yelling Indians, all had served as an equalizer that makes all kinds of men brothers under the skin.

In the beginning the herds were not large, although by the 1870s as many as five thousand or more longhorns were strung out in a single drive, requiring from a dozen to twenty cowboys to handle them. Experience and necessity brought about changes. When only a small number of cowboys had been required, each man was required to be responsible for his own grub and camp cooking. His grub and gear were packed on his extra saddlehorse. But as the herds and number of cowboys and their duties increased, it was found necessary to greatly increase the number of saddlehorses for each man; and a grub and gear cart was added to each outfit. Because of the route they had to travel, these were sturdy carts with two extra-large wheels, and were usually drawn by two or four well-domesticated oxen, driven by the camp cook. This conveyance served to transport food as well as the blankets and other sheer necessities for the crew. As the numbers of the crews increased, and the trails became cut wider and deeper by the hoofs of the thousands of longhorns, the grub cart led to a larger and more completely equipped camp wagon, which in time became the famous chuck wagon of the big cattle outfits on the northern plains.

The drover was the most important member of every sizable trail herd outfit that headed north from Texas, and this custom persisted through the era of the cattle barons on the northern plains. In the trail-drive days the drover was always the top man, and he was the one who handled the business part of the undertaking. He collected the money when the cattle were sold, and paid off the cowboys. All payments were generally in gold. The Texans did not like paper money, for the memory was

"Working a Herd"–EDWARD BOREIN

still fresh in their minds of the time when the Confederate money they had earned and saved during the war had suddenly become worth no more than the paper on which it had been printed. Payment for a large herd amounted to a lot of bulk and weight in gold coins, and a drover needed a man of the highest dependability, and handy with a six-shooter, to be around if needed. The "trail boss" or "wagon boss" was such a man. He served as the No. 2 man in running the big outfits, and in later years he took the place of the drover.

It was around the cowboys' cook and his grub wagon, however, that one of the classic traditions of the cowboy world was created. It appears that from the beginning this character was an extraordinary human being. Generally older than the average cowboy, he was invariably by nature an unsociable individual with a temperament that was pugnaciously independent as well as uniquely eccentric. But he could never be so bad that even the toughest cowboys did not hold him in a high degree of apparent respect, particularly on a trail drive or roundup. When out of hearing distance they called him the "old woman" or "old lady" or other names unfit to print; but the food he served, no matter how bad it might be, was the only food to be had, and hungry cowboys' stomachs had a way of dictating attitudes toward the only hand that fed them. The grub that the trail-driving cowboys ate was invariably just plain bad,

"Trailing Longhorns North"–NICK EGGENHOFER–Miss Deborah Goppert

"Fight in a Frontier Town"—FRANK TENNEY JOHNSON

washed down with big tin cupfuls of equally bad acid-strong coffee, and then all churned up by long hours of intensive activity on the hurricane deck of the cow pony saddle. This was one of the best ways on earth for any man to get periodic dyspepsia, heartburn, or the burps; and relief from "Cookie's" private box of first-aid remedies was a matter of being on good relationships with the old buzzard. There was never a cowboy between Texas and Montana who wasn't at some time faced with a situation in which he badly needed something that Cookie had stashed away among the mysteries of his grub wagon. In addition to the box containing the assortment of patent medicines, pills, salts, quinine, and other advertised remedies for man or beast, he was complete master of the supply of rawhide for mending broken saddle straps, plus rope, horseshoe nails, hammer, extra ammunition, and many other things that when a cowboy a long way from nowhere needed he really needed very badly. To be on good terms with the only man who had what was needed could be very important.

For all the services Cookie performed, a lot of idiosyncrasies could be tolerated. And Cookie was never so dumb that he did not realize he had a rough-and-tough bunch of *hombres* to feed as well as deal with, and the best plan for preserving a comfortable relationship with such a gang was to keep them in a state of awe and respectful anticipation of friendly favors. This became the pattern for their special profession, and it lasted as long as there were cowboys to be fed.

On the other hand, the drovers came to realize the importance of having a good cook. For a bunch of cowboys to come in at the end of a long, hard day in the saddle and find a good meal waiting, could do a lot for any gang of tired and irritable human beings. Cookie also had other duties. He drove the grub wagon (usually through the clouds of dust at the heels of the herd); was expected to have some knowledge of tending to injuries and curing ailments of all kinds for both man and beast; and, in addition, be an all-around handyman. He was even more desirable if he brought along

"A Recruit from Civilization"–FREDERIC REMINGTON

"Camp Wagon on the Trail" (c. 1870)

a guitar, and on an occasional evening when his duties as cook were over he would provide the music for a few songs, religious or ribald, that the cowboys liked best to sing. For all these varied talents and accomplishments, Cookie was a very important member of the crew and was paid somewhat more than the cowboys received.

Another important part of the trail outfit were the two "point riders," who rode at the front of the long-strung-out herd to keep them going in the right direction. This took one rider on each side of the lead animals. When the trail was obvious or well marked by having been traveled by previous herds, the leaders needed little guidance, although it was nothing extraordinary when for some unknown reason the animals might decide to lead the herd in an entirely different direction. There were also times when for one reason or another the course of the herd had to be changed. The leaders were generally obedient, although they resented being crowded or having any of the other herd animals trying to get ahead of them. The lead oxen were generally old animals that had been well domesticated and well trained to be docile and obedient. Occasionally there was a self-appointed leader of a herd, although these generally had an obstinate disposition and frequently had to be guided by the point riders. More often the lead animals were oxen that were returned to Texas and made so many round trips that they knew the whole route as well as any veteran point rider, and became familiar pets of the cowboys.

Not all of the drovers ran their trail drives in the same way, although they learned the same lessons from experience, and operations became much the same. The qualifications of all the cowboys were much the same; and the drover might put two of his outfit on point-riding one day, and on other duties the next.

The number of cowboys stationed in pairs to ride one on each side along the long line of cattle was determined by the drover, although it was on the basis of a rule-of-thumb average of about 300 to 350 animals per 2 men. These cowboys were known as the "swing riders," and it was their duty to keep the cattle moving in some semblance of a line and to keep individuals or small groups from breaking away and possibly leading the rest of the herd in a wrong direction. These strays had to be promptly put back into line. There was occasionally a persistent troublemaker, who after too many obnoxious incidents would be ordered by the drover to be shot; and thus it provided a hearty meal or so of fresh beef for the cowboys, with the rest left for the coyotes.

Back at the end of the long line followed the "tail riders," whose duty it was to keep the stragglers from dropping too far behind, and to protect the rear from attack by Indians. Also following the herd was the grub wagon and the extra saddlehorses for the cowboys. The extra saddlehorses were called the *remuda*, which was Spanish for remount. They were also called "cavvy," derived from *caballado* (horse herd). In

"Point Rider"–EDWARD BOREIN

some instances the cowboys with a large herd would each have as many as six or more remounts, which meant that the *remuda* might consist of as many as fifty to a hundred extra horses. They would be under the charge and responsibility of one or two horse wranglers and were usually herded off to one side when traveling, to avoid some of the dense cloud of thick dust that was stirred up by the large herd of slowly moving cattle. Sometimes the dust was so dense that it was impossible to see in any direction, and the horses did not like to travel in such a cloud of dust. Various other duties also fell to the wranglers besides taking care of the horses. They acted as general handymen around the camps, including chopping wood or gathering dry buffalo or cattle dung "chips" with which to build the smelly fires over which Cookie prepared the meals. The "chips" made a pretty good fire, and the smell helped to keep mosquitoes away; but everybody was more pleased when there was something else over which to cook a supper or early-morning breakfast.

As soon as there was enough daylight to see to build a fire, Cookie was up and getting breakfast started. It was about the time that the cattle were getting onto their feet after a night's rest and ready to look for some grass for a breakfast of their own. The night herders were alert to get the herd grazing leisurely in the desired direction. At the same time the horse wranglers would be getting the saddle bunch herded in handy to the grub wagon and held inside an improvised "rope corral," where the cowboys could quietly pick their mounts for another day in the saddle. The first chore would be to line out the herd and get it moving, slowly enough to permit some grazing and to let the grub wagon and *remuda* fall in at the rear without too much difficulty.

The life of a cowboy on an early-day trail drive north from Texas was more of an ordeal than just a way to make a living—and small recompense he received for

"Saddle Bunch (Remuda)"–EDWARD BOREIN

"The Horse Wrangler"–EDWARD BOREIN–Hammer Galleries, N.Y.

his labor. There were times when the intense heat made it a hell on earth; and the powder-fine dust stirred up by hundreds of longhorn hoofs covered riders and horses alike, saturated a cowboy's clothing clear to the skin, sticking to the bodies of man and beast like mud. At times such as this the traveling was usually across regions where the watering places were far apart and the source of supply was so limited that only a part of a herd could drink at the same time—and the water was unfit for any man to drink. These circumstances tended to disorganize the normal movement of the herd, and added considerably to the cowboys' work as well as aggravating the temperaments of both man and beast. The accumulation of sweat and fatigue, endless days in the saddle, day after day and night after night, dust and rain, swimming muddy rivers, and other hazards were enough to blister the soul of any human being. Twenty, thirty, forty or more days of this got to be old stuff and hard to take.

Every man in one of these outfits was pretty rough and tough in character, or he wouldn't have been there. It was only human for temperaments to flare to explosive proportions. But there was no place for a dissident to go, to find some relaxation and escape from it all—until the end of the long trail was reached. That there were fights and unrecorded fatal incidents is only natural. But in spite of it all, the herds went through to their appointed destinations. And prompted by the first successful trail drives, a considerable number of Texans promptly became energetically engaged in organizing further roundups of longhorns to be driven to the markets in the North.

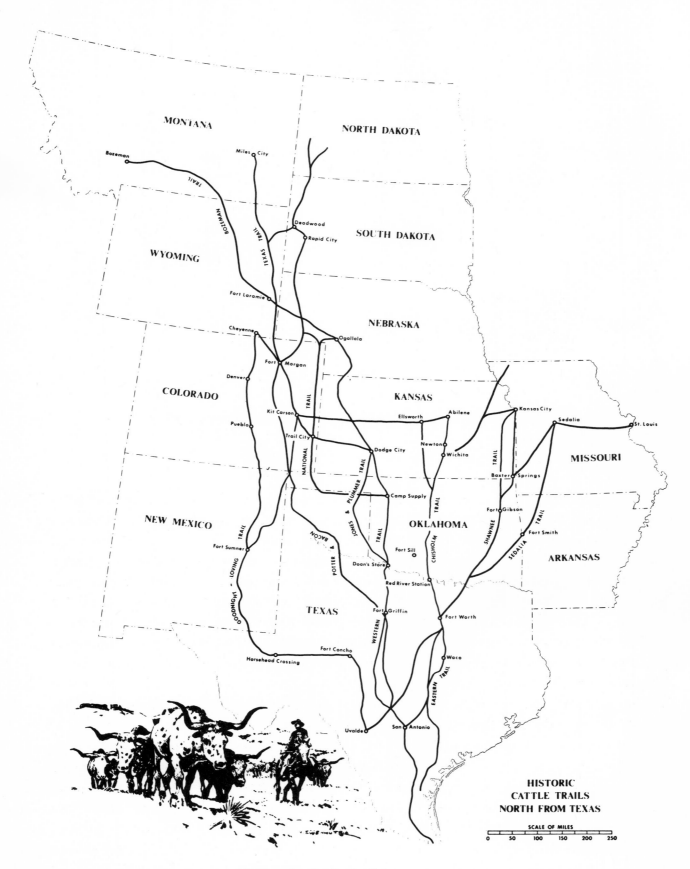

MONTANA

NORTH DAKOTA

Bozeman

Miles City

SOUTH DAKOTA

Deadwood

Rapid City

WYOMING

Fort Laramie

NEBRASKA

Cheyenne

Ogallala

Fort Morgan

Denver

COLORADO

KANSAS

Kansas City

Ellsworth

Abilene

Sedalia

St. Louis

Kit Carson

Pueblo

Trail City

Dodge City

Newton

Wichita

MISSOURI

Baxter Springs

Camp Supply

Fort Gibson

NEW MEXICO

Fort Sill

OKLAHOMA

Fort Smith

Fort Sumner

Doan's Store

ARKANSAS

Red River Station

TEXAS

Fort Griffin

Fort Worth

Fort Concho

Waco

Horsehead Crossing

Uvalde

San Antonio

BOZEMAN TRAIL

TEXAS TRAIL

NATIONAL TRAIL

JONES & PLUMMER TRAIL

POTTER & BACON TRAIL

GOODNIGHT - LOVING TRAIL

WESTERN TRAIL

CHISHOLM TRAIL

SHAWNEE TRAIL

SEDALIA TRAIL

EASTERN TRAIL

HISTORIC
CATTLE TRAILS
NORTH FROM TEXAS

SCALE OF MILES
0   50   100   150   200   250

"Historic Cattle Trails"

Chapter 10

THE CHISHOLM TRAIL

Of all the historic trails over which the hundreds of thousands of Texas longhorns were driven northward into Yankeeland during the brief period immediately following the Civil War, the Chisholm Trail was the first of importance and became the most famous. However, like so many other episodes in the early history of the West, there has been considerable controversy involving this well-used cattle route through the wilderness. With all its human hardships, drama, and significant contribution to empire-building, even the name of the trail and the exact route it followed have been challenged and in dispute, as long ago as by some of the men who claimed to have participated in its cattle drives.

In 1866 it was decided to push a railroad westward from Kansas City (Westport), Missouri. It was to be known as the Kansas Pacific Railway, and its building was to be part of the development of the great plains, which was witnessing a tremendous migration of home-seeking settlers. Early the following summer a construction headquarters was established in about the center of Kansas. Here a few dirt-roofed huts were built alongside the tracks to serve as warehouses for the supplies for the construction work farther west. More and more immigrant settlers had continued coming out into the area by wagon, and it was anticipated that the railroad would bring many more, together with all the things needed to sustain development of the country. Thus the town of Abilene was born.

It is doubtful if much, or any, serious consideration had originally been given by the railroad people to the possibility of providing cattle transportation facilities back East as part of the over-all development program. There was a small stockyard and beef-processing plant in Kansas City, as well as in St. Louis, and a larger one in Chicago, although all the talk and thought of transportation was from east to west. But there was at least one man who had different ideas. This is where ambitious and energetic young Joseph G. McCoy came onto the scene. He realized that Abilene was the nearest point on the railroad in a direct line north from the area where most of the Texas cattle drives were originating. It was only about eight hundred miles by trail from San Antonio. With this in mind he set out to capitalize on the situation.

"Texas Longhorns enroute to Abilene" (1867)

There was no established cattle trail from Texas to Abilene, and there was no railroad equipment suitable for transporting longhorns on the Kansas Pacific Railway. Nor was there any assurance that any of the Texas trail herds could be diverted to the insignificant little construction camp known as Abilene. But with forthright determination and a large amount of gambling spirit, McCoy set about building cattle-loading pens alongside the railroad tracks, as well as pursuing the problem of convincing the railroad officials of the economic desirability of using their freight trains to carry cattle back to Kansas City rather than "dead-heading" them back empty. With cattle pens in the process of being built and the railroad officials willing to be convinced, there still remained the important problem of having cattle to fill the pens, and having cattle buyers on hand to purchase the longhorns and consign them to the railroad for shipment. But McCoy had planned the whole thing very carefully. He sent representatives to the Texas areas where the trail herds were being organized, and others rode out across the country to meet herds that were already on their way to possible markets, to induce the drovers to take their cattle to the new shipping point on the Kansas Pacific Railway.

Results were not long in being realized. The first herd to arrive at Abilene was intercepted on its way north. It had been driven from Texas by a Mr. Thompson and sold in the region of the Indian Nation to the northern buying combine of Smith, McCord, and Chandler, and driven by them to Abilene before the construction of the stock pens was completed. Shortly afterward a second herd arrived. This one was owned by Col. O. W. Wheeler, Wilson, and Hicks, and had been en route to California, but was induced to change its course and go to Abilene. The first shipment of twenty cars was made over the Kansas Pacific Railway on September 5, 1867. Others followed, to the extent that approximately thirty-five thousand head of longhorns trail-driven from Texas came into Abilene for railroad shipment before the end of that first year.[19]

Generally speaking, the Chisholm Trail extended in a northerly direction from San Antonio, via Fort Worth, then Red River Station on the Texas border, and then on across present Oklahoma and Kansas to Abilene. The cattle trail took its name from an upper section of less that 150 miles that had been previously used by a noted frontier character by the name of Jesse Chisholm. His father was a Scotsman and his mother a mixed-blood Cherokee Indian. A well-known guide, trail builder, and one of the most influential of the earlier-day traders of the Southwest, Jesse Chisholm had used the trail adopted by the cattle drives for trading with Indians and buffalo hunters. When the cattle herds came up from Texas to Abilene the drovers chose to follow Chisholm's trail from the crossing on the Cimarron River at a place near present Dover, Oklahoma, to near the present site of Wichita, Kansas. Although Jesse Chisholm was never a cowboy nor in any way interested in the cattle business, except for the oxen that were yoked to his wagons loaded with trade goods, his name was given to the most famous of all the early-day trails of the longhorns.

Those early shipments of cattle from Abilene were a great step forward in the establishment of the cattle industry on the northern plains. Not only did they establish the feasibility of shipping beef cattle to markets in the East, but they resulted in setting the pattern for frontier cowboy whoopla towns the like of which had never been known before.

The fact that some 35,000 head of longhorns were trail-driven up to Abilene during about half of the first year meant that at least 232 working cowboys plus 35 or more drovers came with them to the little budding town alongside the railroad

"Abilene Passenger Depot" (1870)

"'Cow Punchers'" at Work–Abilene" (1870)

tracks. These were mostly, if not all, Texans who only about two years before had been serving with the Confederate Cavalry or other branches of the Southern Army. They were still naturally bitter in defeat, and coming as they were with about all they had, to sell to their seemingly prosperous victors, did not help their feelings. But they were well received. They were weary from the long ordeals of the trail drive through the inhospitable wilderness. They now had money to spend and the urge to do so, and the places that had hastily been prepared for their special entertainment offered a wide-open welcome for them to come in and indulge. There were also northern men from the railroad construction camps, and others who had come to settle in the country, who had served in the Union Army. They too went to the places of entertainment. Human nature being as it is, these places became a neutral meeting ground, where all the bitter memories of war were drowned in a few drinks of cheap whiskey, or submerged by some honky-tonk music and a dance with a painted lady, and new friendships were made.

It is probably true that since the building of the great pyramids in Egypt, there has been a class of merchants who appear whenever there is a big construction job in progress, and they hastily establish drinking and gambling places, dance halls with female company available, as well as lodging and eating places. When the boom is over, these camp followers move on, usually to leave only the ghosts of their efforts behind; although sometimes, particularly in the early days of the American West, their makeshift establishments became the forerunners of prosperous and sedate communities. Sometimes a bartender became a dignified banker, mayor, or state governor. The same was true of some of those Texas cowboys who drove the longhorns up the trails and decided to stay and become a part of the life on the northern plains.

The cowboys who had driven the herds of half-wild longhorns northward through the wilderness were mostly young men, prematurely aged by a war and its aftermaths that had given them little more than an indifference to life and the future. But they had become men of iron during the trail drives. By the time they reached Abilene it required no urging for them to plunge with reckless abandon into the frontier gala that had been specially prepared for just such circumstances. It was all very new to them, from the railroad with its steam engines to the saloons and the brazenly flamboyant women in the dance halls. The cowboys were equal to handling a wild mustang, a renegade longhorn, or an attack by hostile Comanches; but the entertainments offered in Abilene were something quite different. These Texas cowboys came dusty and dirty, unshaven and unsheared, and their clothing was grimy and torn. The cattle sold, they were without responsibilities. They had received what was perhaps the first civilian wage money they ever had. The Yankee money in their pockets seemed like a fortune; and under the sun- and sweat-tanned skin of each muscular body was a perfectly normal human being. Once they got the hang of standing up to a bar and ordering man-sized drinks of whiskey that was made for profit rather than discriminating taste, then the other diversions just came naturally. They learned quickly; and while this did not necessarily set the pattern for their lives, it did set a pattern for what happened at the end of the long trail drives from Texas. Here, also, there arose a feeling that Texas and Texans shared a mutual part in the development of the frontier West, which was far more important than who had won or lost the recent war.

Some of the cowboys who brought the trail herds into Abilene found temporary or permanent employment in handling the longhorns in outlying holding areas after

"Dance Hall–Abilene" (c. 1870)

"A Rough Character"–EDWARD W. KEMBLE

the herd was sold, or around the cattle yards and loading pens, from which the cattle were put aboard the railroad cars for shipment. The latter chore presented a problem, for the naturally obstinate longhorns objected to being prodded into entering the close confines of the cattle cars. To aid in this, long poles with sharply pointed front ends were devised with which to punch and hurry the animals along, as illustrated on page 100. It was from this that the cowboys detailed to such duty came to be known as "cow punchers"—an expression that came to be wrongly used for any and all cowboys.

The Kansas and Pacific Railway brought a steadily increasing flow of folks who were far less colorful and dramatic than cowboys from Texas. Most of the newcomers were families, with plows and other farm tools, who came to become permanent home-

"Stopped by Buffalo" (1870s)

steaders on the land around the new towns and along the railroad. They kept close to the towns, for there was still serious Indian trouble to be considered. Most of the signle men stopped in Abilene, to look for work as carpenters or in other trades, although some opened little shops or stores. The homesteaders came in such numbers and settled on the land so rapidly around Abilene that it soon began to present a serious problem in bringing the trail herds in to the stockyards, or to the loading pens alongside the railroad.

By 1870 there were three hundred thousand Texas longhorns driven up the Chisholm Trail to Abilene, and the number rapidly increased. For that large number of cattle to be driven across any man's farmland would completely cut it to pieces and ruin his crop for a long time to come. The congestion of Texas longhorns became so great, and the problem with the homesteaders became so serious, that it was necessary for McCoy and his associates to build new stockyards and loading pens at a place called Ellsworth, about seventy miles farther west on the railroad. From that time on, Abilene went into a rapid decline as the cowboy and cattle-shipping capital of the West. This was the first occasion when the inexorable juggernaut of human migration to the West and the spreading settlement by homesteaders exerted the social pressures that were to slowly but irresistibly push the cattle industry off the map.

By 1871 there were over half a million head of cattle driven up the Chisholm Trail. During that year, also, the Atchison, Topeka & Santa Fe Railway was built from Emporia to Newton, Kansas, about sixty miles south of Abilene; and shipping pens were built there to handle the herds. In most respects Newton was much like Abilene, but what Newton lacked in size it made up for in hectic violence. It was here that an element of the West turned bawdry, wild, and woolly. It has been claimed that during Newton's brief existence more men died of violent deaths in the same length of time than in any other frontier cattle town.

"Dodge City, Kansas" (1878)

The business of handling Texas longhorns steadily moved westward with the extension of the railroads and settlement of the country by homesteaders. The center of activity in loading the cattle for railroad shipment eastward shifted several times. Wichita, Caldwell, and Great Bend had their day in claiming credit for being the "cowboy capital" of the West. Each time the railroad shipping town shifted, all the riffraff of boom-town followers, saloon keepers, gamblers, and dance hall girls moved with the tide, and accumulated. The situation moved rapidly.

By July 1872 the chief engineer of the Atchison, Topeka & Santa Fe Railway, with some other interested individuals, laid out a new town in the southwestern part of Kansas. It was a short distance from U. S. Army post Fort Dodge, which was under the command of Col. Richard I. Dodge; and the new town was named "Dodge City." The "town company" that promoted the establishment of the new town consisted of Colonel Dodge; Maj. E. B. Kirk, the Army quartermaster; and several other officers, as well as Robert M. Wright, who for a good many years had been a very successful frontier trader, freighter, and dealer in buffalo hides on a large scale. The area already had a particularly dramatic past history, and the new town was destined to quickly become widely known as not only the most exciting cowboy capital of them all, but also as "the wickedest town on earth."

For a good many years the large wagon trains had traveled the Santa Fe Trail past the location selected for the building of Dodge City. Thirty to eighty or even more wagons, each hauled by up to six or more oxen, traveled together for protection, for that section of the trail went through "bad" Indian country. It was the hunting ground of the Kiowas, Arapahoes, and southern Cheyenne, as well as the white men; and it was known to the old wagon train men as the *hornodo de muerte* (journey of death). Nowhere were more heinous Indian atrocities committed or more commonplace.

Selected as a temporary terminus at the end-of-steel of the railroad, Dodge City was about three hundred miles west of Kansas City and one hundred miles from the Colorado border. It was in one of the greatest buffalo hunting areas of the West.

Robert M. Wright had lived among the buffalo and their hunters through the previous fifteen years and estimated the number at around twenty-five million. Wright himself shipped over two hundred thousand buffalo hides during the first winter after the railroad reached the newly founded town. "And I think there were at least as many more shipped; besides two hundred cars of hindquarter and two cars of tongues. Dodge had become a very busy place before the depot could be built. The streets were lined with wagons, bringing in hides and meat, and getting supplies from early morning to late at night," he states in his informative book, *Dodge City: The Cowboy Capital.*[20]

It took a mighty tough and pugnacious breed of white man to make his habitat in the region in which Dodge City was situated, both before and after the town was founded. Dodge quickly became the rendezvous and center of business and social activity of a large number of individuals who were equal to any challenge the country might produce. Beside the buffalo hunters and their skinners and wagon men, there were trail freighters, bull whackers, wagon bosses, guides, Army scouts, gamblers, bartenders, prostitutes, gold seekers, and, of course, the railroad construction crews, cattle buyers, cow punchers, and the large number of cowboys. It was probably the most motley, extraordinary assemblage of rough characters ever gathered on any frontier. "All the wild and woolly men from hundreds of miles gathered at Dodge City, getting drunk and riding up and down the street as fast as a horse could go; firing a six-shooter and whooping like wild Indians were favorite pastimes, exciting, innocent, and amusing."[21] But there were plenty of recorded fatal shootings; and as

"A Texan Cowboy"
−FREDERIC REMINGTON

"A Shattered Idol"−FREDERIC REMINGTON

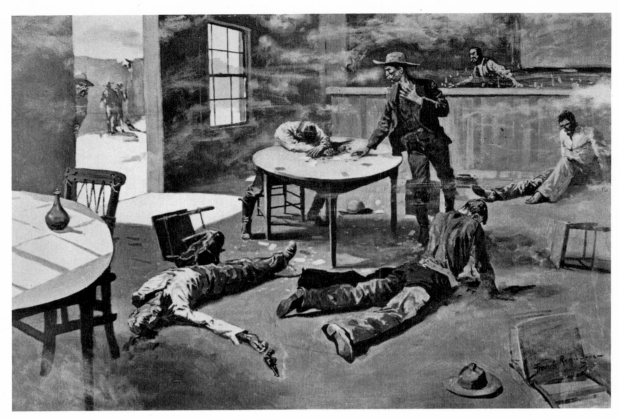

"A Misdeal"–FREDERIC REMINGTON

the town grew, it took some of the most noted of the law-enforcement men of the West to keep a faint semblance of order. The town's "peace commission" at one time included such names as Bat Masterson, Wyatt Earp, Luke Short, Neil Brown, and Charlie Bassett.

The wild and wicked reputation that Dodge City gained for itself cannot be blamed on the cowboys who brought the big herds up from Texas to that important marketplace at the end of the railroad. After the long, grueling weeks in the saddle they were eager to join in the diversions that were offered; but since they were unaccustomed to such exciting entertainments, it was easy for them to get in trouble. However, with the small pay received from their labor, they were certainly not the biggest spenders in town.

For a few of Dodge City's earliest years the great herds of buffalo were the source of a large share of the business activity and prosperity of the town. Buffalo hunting was a regular occupation for a considerable number of men, and the traffic in buffalo hides and meat was a business of vast proportions. It was during the period of about 1872 to 1880 that the buffalo were virtually exterminated on the western plains, and Dodge City was the principal center of this traffic. When the source of supply began to fail, however, a substitute was almost immediately on hand, with the cowboys coming to Dodge driving the big herds of longhorns from Texas.

The first cattle drives that ended at Dodge City, according to Robert M. Wright, were in 1875, when nearly 250,000 longhorns were driven up from Texas. In 1877 there were over 300,000, and the number increased each year until the drives reached approximately half a million head. Dodge held the lead in this trade until 1886. According to Wright there were more cattle driven to Dodge City, during every year

"Argument with the Town Marshal"–FREDERIC REMINGTON

"The Longhorn Cattle Sign"—FREDERIC REMINGTON

the town was engaged in the trade, than any other town; and during those years Dodge was the greatest cattle market in the world.

When the cattle reached the railroad, the buyers paid around eight dollars a head for yearlings and seven dollars for heifers.[22] Generally a whole herd was involved in the deal, and there was some bargaining. Considering the number of longhorns driven north each year, the dollars that changed hands ran into Millions. Wright estimates, however, that not more than half of the money got back to Texas. A large part of the money that was spent in Dodge City went with reckless abandon in the places of entertainment. A good many cowboys, particularly on their first trip north, quickly went through the relatively small amount they received, and then without a dollar had to make the long ride back to Texas to help round up another herd to drive north. After a trip or two a good many of the cowboys learned to either stay away from the gambling places and dance halls or avoid the go-for-broke plunge.

Many of the Texas cowboys who came to Dodge City also stayed in the North once the long drives were over. They worked as cowboys or went into other occupations. There were a lot of cattle-raising projects being started in western Kansas, Colorado, and Nebraska, and a cowboy with a couple of trail drives up from Texas as a background of experience had little difficulty in getting a job with one of the new northern outfits. In fact, the cattle-raising industry on the western plains was just beginning to take preference over shipment of the longhorns to the eastern stockyards and slaughterhouses, to which the railroads had been taking them. There were plenty of cheap Texas longhorns to start a cattle-raising project on the free range where the buffalo once ranged in profusion, and more and more industrious individuals were getting into the business.

There were, of course, other cattle trails in addition to the Chisholm and Dodge City trails. There was the old Shawnee Trail, which ran from a long way south of San Antonio, along the Eastern Trail up to Fort Worth; then crossed the Red River at

"Trail Herd at Dawn"–EDWARD BOREIN–Courtesy Dr. H. D. Burtness

Preston, well east of the Chisholm crossing; then curved northeast to Fort Gibson, northward into Kansas at Baxter Springs, and on to Kansas City. There was also a branch-off, bearing east above Fort Gibson, that went into Missouri at its southwestern corner and up to Sedalia, where it turned due east to St. Louis. The Western Trail extended northwest from San Antonio to Fort Griffin and northward, crossing the Red River at Doan's Store, then on to Camp Supply, and to Dodge City. This was also known as the Dodge City Trail, and it was later extended northward to Ogallala, Nebraska, where one branch turned northwest, while the main trail continued northward across South Dakota up into North Dakota. The fourth and westernmost of the main cattle trails north from Texas was the Goodnight-Loving Trail. Charles Goodnight was an ex-Texas Ranger, and Oliver Loving was an important cattleman in southwestern Texas. The trail that was named for them followed the old California Trail from Uvalde northwest to Horsehead Crossing on the Pecos River; then swung north into New Mexico to Fort Sumner; on into Colorado to Pueblo, Denver, and on to Cheyenne, Wyoming, with a branch cutting off to Kit Carson, and on northward across Wyoming to Miles City, Montana. All of these four main trails had branches that cut off to places where there were potential demands for cattle. There were also a few other trails of lesser importance.

Charles Goodnight and Oliver Loving are recognized as two of the most important individuals in the early development of the cattle-raising industry on the western plains north of Texas. Goodnight operated mostly west of the shipping points on the railroads, pioneering his own markets rather than driving his herds to the buying places for shipment to the eastern stockyards. His first important market was the government contractor's at Fort Sumner (Bosque Redondo) in east-central New Mexico, where the Army was obligated to supply meat rations to the Navajo tribesmen concentrated on the reservation after the Navajo had been defeated in a long campaign in which "Kit" Carson had taken a leading role. To supply this market, Goodnight pioneered the beginning of the cattle trail that bore his name. As a result he sold many thousands of longhorns at Fort Sumner. He did drive some cattle from his Panhandle ranch to Dodge City, although his greatest interest seems to have been to sell his livestock for cattle-raising ranch projects in eastern Colorado and southeastern Wyoming.

One of the most classic of all the pioneer cattle drives was one from Texas to Virginia City, Montana, when that remote frontier place became a gold-discovery boom town. A young Ohio-born overland freighter by the name of Nelson Story had joined the gold rush to Virginia City in 1863. He found no gold, but he realized the opportunity of making some substantial money from bringing in fresh meat on-the-hoof, and in 1865 he went to Texas to round up some longhorns. The following spring he started on the return journey with about six hundred head of the Spanish cattle.

From the beginning, Nelson Story was beset with all sorts of trouble, with both the cattle and Indians, but he and his cowboys finally managed to get the herd through to Fort Laramie, in Wyoming Territory. He then headed north over the newly laid-out stage and freight Bozeman Trail, which wound its way northwest across the inhospi-

"The Trail Boss"–EDWARD BOREIN

table wilderness that was dominated by the most warlike of all the northern Indians, the Sioux. The Sioux were at the time on a rampage of vengeance against all white men in the Big Horn country through which Story had to travel, and he was warned by Col. H. B. Carrington, of the Army, not to make any attempt to get the cattle through. The Powder River country was full of Sioux, and it would be suicide for the whole group. However, with his twenty-seven riders, all armed with new Remington rapid-fire, breech-loading rifles, Story set out with his herd of longhorns along the dangerous trail. They had some serious engagements with the Sioux; but only one of the cowboys was killed and two severely wounded. Also, winter caught them, which compounded the difficulties in handling the Spanish cattle, which were native to a warm climate, and the snow and cold added to the hardships of the men as well. How they managed to get the herd through to Virginia City is little short of a frontier miracle. The success of the venture was due only to the extraordinary determination of Nelson Story and his cowboys. The longhorns were finally brought to the desired destination on December 3, 1866. It was the first cattle drive from Texas into Montana, and the cattle were sold at a worthy profit. Neither Story nor anyone else made another attempt until in the late 1870s.

The western migration of homesteaders and town builders was spreading like a tide across the great plains, and it was this fact more than anything else that was bringing about the great transition that was taking place in the cattle industry. Also, the vast open range of the North was starting to become a stock-breeding and raising section; and this new territory was to become the setting for the flowering of the American cowboy as he has been immortalized in history.

"John Ermine, Northern Frontiersman"–FREDERIC REMINGTON

Chapter 11

THE GREAT TRANSITION

A great many important changes were destined to take place in the American West shortly after the end of the Civil War. Virtually every aspect of life on the great plains was to be affected. The transition was to be both extensive and conclusive. The multitudinous, wild-natured Texas longhorns were destined to become as nearly extinct as the buffalo that had been a resident of the region for thousands of years, and the granite-tough trail drivers would end their relatively brief roles in the dramatic extravaganza of the passing frontier. Even the Indian, to whom the whole West had been his ancestral homeland, was to be deprived not only of his land but of all his traditional culture and made a captive of the foreign intruders.

All these changes were to be brought about by what became a cliché, "the taming of the West." The whole thing had started in a small way in the late eighteenth century, when a few English and French adventurers began traveling west to develop the fur trade; and this led to the first trickle of covered-wagon pioneers, who around 1825 became the vanguard of the western migration of homeseekers. In 1832 artist George Catlin went up the Missouri River on the first passenger- and supply-carrying boat, to paint and study the Indians in their still-primitive state. In what Catlin wrote to accompany his pictures he made a prophetic prediction of what was to follow in the wake of those first immigrants he was privileged to observe. He described it as "the approach of the bustling, busy, talkative, elated and exultant white man . . . the splendid juggernaut rolling on with its splendid desolation . . . the certain approach of this overwhelming system which will inevitably march on and prosper."

A generation or so later, the California gold rush added to this westward migration; although it was not until after the widespread interruption of the Civil War, and substantially aided by the very important building of the railroads, that the real migration of human beings developed into a full flood. It was this great number of homeseeking families, along with mercenary-minded builders of little towns, all aided by the railroads, that were responsible for the taming and the great transition in the West —certainly one of the most extraordinary episodes in history.

Never before had there been such a large and so heterogeneous a mass of people migrate into such a richly habitable wilderness. The immigrants were principally from the states east of the Mississippi River, although many represented new arrivals from practically every nation of Europe, and there was a sprinkling of Asians. A considerable number spoke only the language of their motherland, although all were trying to learn English as best they could. All faced common difficulties and dangers. They had no common leader, but shared the common aspiration to find new homes and a new life for themselves and their future generations. They were also bound by a common desire to grow up peacefully together and to make the soil and all the natural resources of this new land beneficial to their labors.

There were other factors that contributed to the great transition and that were to directly affect the whole cattle industry as well as the type of cowboys and the handling of the herds. The wagon trains of pioneer families that had moved out over the Oregon Trail, even before the California gold rush, had used farm-raised oxen and had been accompanied by milking and breeding cattle, all of Durham and other eastern shorthorn varieties. This was indeed a vastly different scene than *conquistadors* driving their obdurate Spanish longhorns. But from the small and unromantic beginnings of these early American pioneers, some modestly sizable herds of "American" cattle were developed in remote places in Wyoming and Montana, as well as Oregon, as early as the 1840s and 1850s; and their kind were destined to prosper and dominate throughout the western prairies.

It was widely recognized that the barnyard types of American shorthorns were far superior table beef than the half-wild Spanish longhorns. But the shorthorns were limited in number, and there were widespread and serious doubts that they could survive the long, cold winters roaming out on the inhospitable open ranges of the northern plains, without having the shelter, care, and feeding they were accustomed to

"Opening up the Cattle Country on the Northern Plains"—FREDERIC REMINGTON

"*Riding Herd in the Rain*"–FREDERIC REMINGTON–Whitney Gallery, Cody, Wyo.

around a family farmyard. However, there was a story that received wide circulation that strongly tended to refute the feeling that the shorthorn was lacking in rugged characteristics. It had been reported that an overland freighter who was caught out on the prairie of the Northwest by the early coming of a winter snowstorm in desperation unhitched all his shorthorn oxen and abandoned them to hurry on to find shelter at the nearest human habitation. Not until the following spring was the freighter able to return to the place where he had left everything to save his own life. He took back with him some new oxen with the hope of salvaging at least part of his freight cargo. However, to his great surprise he found all of his original oxen near the big wagon, having not only survived through the winter on the buffalo grass of the prairie, but also in excellent condition. There is no proof that this story is based on an actual incident, although there is no reason to doubt it because of the many thousands of shorthorn cattle that in later years wintered successfully under similar conditions.

It was not unusual for some of the more important of the early fur traders to have American oxen and milk cows around their fortified trading posts. These had been brought out over the trails from the East long before the first longhorns were brought north from Texas. There were isolated instances, even in the very northern part of the northern plains, where more or less serious efforts were made to establish cattle-raising projects. One of the most important of these was in what is today the western part of the state of Montana. There, in the Deer Lodge Valley, as early as 1853, one Johnny Grant, the son of a Hudson's Bay Fur Company trader, began building a herd of shorthorn cattle. That was thirty-six years before Montana became a state. He went into the business in a serious manner. In 1866 Grant sold the ranch and some four thousand head of cattle to a Danish immigrant by the name of Conrad Kohrs, who carried on for a long time in an admirable way.

Another early pioneer in the shorthorn cattle business on the northern part of the northern plains was Elias W. Whitcomb. In 1858, thirty-two years before Wyoming became a state, this man was in charge of twelve hundred eastern work oxen at famous Fort Laramie on the Oregon Trail. These oxen were owned by the overland freighting organization of Russell, Majors & Wadell, with whom William F. Cody (later known as "Buffalo Bill") had his first employment on the western plains. Elias Whitcomb also owned six four-yoke ox teams of his own, which he hired out to the government at 10 dollars a day. At that time there were no range cattle in the region, but Whitcomb started his own ranch for the breeding and raising of shorthorn stock. He was successful in the undertaking, and in 1880 he sold the ranch and cattle for 250,000 dollars—which was a lot of money at that time.

The eventual shift to raising shorthorns, because of the far superior quality of beef they provided, was a natural one, which was hindered only because of the lack of availability of this variety of cattle in sufficient numbers to establish sizable herds. But the shift was anticipated long before it happened, as indicated by Joseph G. McCoy in his *Historic Sketches of the Cattle Trade:* "The Durham or 'short-horned' blood is sought by breeders . . . it is a well-established fact they can more easily be fattened on corn. . . . In Colorado it is made by statute a punishable offense to permit a Texas, or scur bull, to run at large, and ranchmen are authorized to shoot down such whenever and wherever they may meet them upon the commons. . . . Indeed, it is astonishing, as well as highly encouraging, to note the marked improvement in color, form and weight, arising from a cross of Texas cows and Durham bulls . . . the ordinary observer will scarce believe that the cross, or half-breed, has any Texan blood in it. But little trace of the mother is transmitted to her offspring which sell upon the eastern market as well as other Durham grades. . . . The interest in thoroughbred short-

"Trailing Texas Cattle"–FREDERIC REMINGTON

"The Roper"–EDWARD BOREIN–Hammer Galleries, N.Y.

horn cattle continually increases, as is plainly indicated by the sales that have occurred."[23]

It remained for the railroads to open the floodgates for the big migration; to populate the West; and to bring about the many changes that were to affect virtually all phases of life, from red men and white men, to animals both wild and domesticated. In the 1860s and 1870s railroads were a new means of transportation. Building them required little time at all, on the pages of history, until that epochal day of May 10, 1869 when the driving of a golden spike at Promontory, Utah, marked the completion of the first transcontinental railroad. The ceremonies of that connecting of the Union Pacific and the Central Pacific resounded throughout the civilized world as a clarion announcement that the American West was open for settlement. It also stimulated the building of other railroads, and branches of railroads, into every section of the land; and everywhere they went they took more and more immigrants to settle, develop, and bring changes to the country.

By the end of the 1870s the St. Louis, Iron Mountain & Southern Railway had linked up at Texarkana with the Texas & Pacific Railway to Fort Worth. This heralded the end of the long trail drives of longhorns out of Texas. Far to the north, across the plains, the Northern Pacific was being pushed westward through Dakota and Montana, bringing the big Chicago stockyards within easy reach of the uppermost part of the northern plains. It was indeed a changing world, particularly for the cattle industry. The big cattle contractors and all buyers of beef were demanding better table meat, and paying by-the-pound rather than by-the-head for what had been cheap and easily available.

Furthermore, the frontier was becoming measured in terms of the settlement of the land by homesteaders and the establishment of small towns. Development of the cattle industry was dependent upon the open plains. From the beginning it had been pushed steadily westward as the rangeland became occupied by these "nesters" (builders of small family nests on the prairies), as the settlers were derogatively known to the cattlemen. When the frontier was pushed back against the Rocky Mountains of Colorado, the trend of things to come turned northward, until it was halted by the serious Indian troubles in the regions of Wyoming and South Dakota. The warlike and powerful Sioux still roamed freely and ruled defiantly from the big bend of the Missouri River westward to the Rockies. It took real courage for any white pioneer to settle in the region; and to protect a grazing herd of cattle on the lush prairie was more than the United States Army could handle at the time. The Battle of the Little Big Horn on June 25, 1876, was not really a test of strength between the Sioux and the Army, although it marked the climax of half a century of bitter and bloody struggle and was in itself a sign of the times. But for a brief time the unfortunate fate of General Custer and all of his men served as a warning to all kinds of immigrants to refrain from venturing into the region.

On the other hand, there was that magic lure of thousands of square miles of grassy prairies, which had provided ideal rangeland for the great herds of buffalo for centuries into the past. There were fortunes to be made in a hundred regions where the free grass spread from horizon to horizon and far beyond, everywhere lying waiting for the first to come and the strongest to stay. It was a land where law and order was more a matter of power than principle. It was a rough country, which called for men strong enough to hold what they wanted to keep. There was plenty of room to create a hundred individual little empires, ruled over by feudal cattle barons, as independent as kings who paid no tributes, each the complete master over his own domain, the

"Short Throw"–EDWARD BOREIN

"A Critical Moment"–FREDERIC REMINGTON

most despotic autocrat in the whole dictionary of American characters. And along with these cattle barons would be their indispensable cowboys, every bit as rugged and individualistic as the man who depended on them to protect and preserve his little empire, and the free grass that turned to gold after every roundup. These were the men who challenged and stood off the most desperate raids the worst of the Indian renegades could launch against them and who met every other challenge that jeopardized the continued success of their cattle-baron master.

The cattle industry in Wyoming Territory was first developed in the area that is today the southeastern section of the state. This was a region particularly suitable for cattle grazing. It lay to the south of Fort Laramie, which was from the earliest days one of the most important military strongholds and supply centers on the Oregon Trail and the northern route via Great Salt Lake to California. Because of the large amount of overland travel that had passed through this hazardous Indian country, there were more than ordinary amounts of U. S. Army units in this area, with the best of the Cavalry centered not only at Fort Laramie but also at nearby Fort Fetterman, Fort D. A. Russell, and Fort Bridger. The presence of the roving Cavalry and a good many veteran Army units had a sobering effect on the Indians, although this did not assure complete safety for settlers or cattlemen.

"Bronco Sam"–EDWARD W. KEMBLE

Another advantage of this Wyoming cattle country was the newly built Union Pacific Railroad and the rapidly growing town of Cheyenne, providing a shipping center with transportation going directly to markets in the East. The first shipment, according to records of the Wyoming Stock Growers Association, was in 1870.[24] It was reported that the shipping facilities were crude and the journey was hard on the animals. But this was the beginning of cattle shipments from the Northwest to the markets in the East, and significantly it involved shorthorns. By 1871, cattle raising had grown considerably, although it was still largely confined to the southeastern region. The official report of the surveyor-general of the Territory of Wyoming for that year reported eight areas in the southeastern section of the territory grazing a total of 54,550 head of cattle. The center of the business activity was the rapidly growing town of Cheyenne. The town's newspaper, the *Daily Leader,* in an article in the issue of April 11, 1872, estimated that the number of cattle in the region had "doubled or increased four times since 1869."

Not only did the Wyoming cattle raisers have the important advantage of almost unlimited areas of free grasslands on which they might expand, as well as easy access to railroad transportation directly to the eastern markets, but there was also the fact that big investors in the East as well as England and Scotland were becoming very interested in the substantial money-making possibilities of the cattle-raising business in the West. Representatives of these financial interests were sent to various parts of the West to investigate and make recommendations. In spite of the continuing Indian troubles in Wyoming, especially in the northern part of the territory, the future ex-

"One of the Boys"–FREDERIC REMINGTON

pansion of the cattle-raising industry in the region was considered the most promising. As a result, substantial investment capital began appearing on the scene. Money became so abundant in Cheyenne that it was talked about as the richest town in the West. The Wyoming Stock Growers Association reported that capitalization in the immediate area was in the neighborhood of one hundred million dollars. This fact becomes even more impressive when one realizes that at this time Wyoming Territory was little more than a wilderness inhabited largely by unfriendly Indians, and Cheyenne was just an overgrown frontier village.

What the cattlemen of southeastern Wyoming wanted and needed more than anything else were more shorthorn stock, for the building of cattle empires on the expansive northern free grazing lands that were waiting to be appropriated. The cattlemen realized that shorthorn beeves were the answer to future success in the cattle-raising industry. The most obvious answer was in Oregon and Washington, which presented a situation that in a good many respects resembled that in Texas following the Civil War. In the Pacific Northwest the shorthorn cattle completely dominated the stock; and the herds had increased to such an extent that the cattlemen were very much in need of an outlet for their surplus. The Oregon Trail, which had its western end in Oregon and over which most of the original shorthorn stock had traveled in earlier days, fortunately crossed the southern part of Wyoming very handy to where the new cattle-raising area was being developed. All that was necessary was to trail-drive the Oregon-Washington cattle back eastward to Wyoming.

Raising shorthorns in the Pacific Northwest had been carried on in a rather back-

East farmyard fashion, from the days of the earliest settlers who went out over the Oregon Trail or came around the Horn by sailing ships. However, following the California gold rush there were several other gold discoveries in the Northwest that sent hundreds of get-rich-quick hopefuls to the scene. These lesser stampedes ranged from the Fraser River in British Columbia to central Idaho, eastern Oregon, and elsewhere. Most of these gold camps were quite successful, and they created a healthy market for fresh beef, which Oregon proceeded to supply. This greatly activated the development of cattle raising, although the momentum that was developed carried over beyond the lifespan of the mining camps and resulted in a great oversupply, which had continued to multiply. Thus it was that the cattle owners in the Northwest were as anxious to sell as the Wyoming cattlemen were to buy.

In 1874 the estimated ninety thousand head of cattle on the ranges of southeastern Wyoming contained a considerable amount of longhorn blood, although most of the Texas bulls had been eliminated. The following year Wyoming cattlemen were in the Pacific Northwest buying large numbers of shorthorns to upgrade their breeding stock. In the issue of May 22, 1875, the newspaper Walla Walla *Union* reported the buying spree of a Wyoming cattleman who was snapping up all the thoroughbred shorthorns he could find with a view to trail-driving them to Wyoming Territory. And shortly afterward the same newspaper reported that a herd of several hundred head of the locally purchased cattle had been started on their way eastward to the new range.[25] This was the beginning of a series of increasingly large shorthorn cattle drives from the Pacific Northwest over the Oregon Trail to Wyoming. The newspapers being published in the various Oregon-Washington areas where these cattle drives originated,

"Moving in the Herd"–W. H. D. KOERNER

"Last of the Longhorns"–N. C. WYETH

recorded in considerable detail the movements of the large drives eastward and provide a far more complete and accurate documentation of the era than that of the earlier drives of longhorns northward out of Texas. Virtually all of the Wyoming-bound cattle were well-bred shorthorns, and the records report that the herds ranged from a few hundred to many thousand.

It was reported that during the year 1880 more than two hundred thousand head of shorthorns were trail-driven eastward out of the Oregon-Washington region, mostly into Wyoming. One of these drives consisted of a thirty-thousand-head herd that was assembled by the active and well-known trail-driving combine of Lang and Ryan, and some interesting statistics were reported on this drive: "To drive these cattle to the Yellowstone country, will require 800 head of horses and the service of 120 men. Most of the 'cowboys' are Kansas men, who have been in the employ of this concern for the past six years. Forty wagons accompany this drive, and about 160 stand of loaded rifles will always be on hand, for about 3000 shots at any band of hostile Indians that might attack them. The drive will be cut up into three squads or bands of cattle, the first lot having two days start on the third . . . and the greatest

"American Cowboy, Eastern Horse, and Shorthorn"–CARL RUNGIUS

body of cattle ever banded together will be slowly marched eastward. Up to the 20th of June the drive will move about nine miles per day, but as summer comes they will decrease it to about five." This account appeared in the *Drover's Journal* (a Chicago publication connected with the Chicago stockyards) on June 10, 1880, and it was copied from the Oregon *Willamette Farmer*, which had lifted it from the *Morning Oregonian*.[26]

The eastward drives from Oregon and Washington in 1882 appear to be the last important ones made. During the approximately seven years that these drives were taking place, the great surplus of shorthorns, which had accumulated in the Pacific Northwest, had been drained to the extent that cattle were becoming relatively scarce, except for the family barnyard bossies. But the cattle that had gone back over the historic Oregon Trail and its northern branch, the Mullin Road from Walla Walla via Fort Missoula to Helena, Great Falls, Livingston, and Cody, contributed in major part to the great transition from longhorns to shorthorns in all the herds on our western plains, even in Texas, where the longhorns had originated. By a long, circuitous route the shorthorn from northern Europe via the eastern sections of America met the longhorn that had originated in southern Europe and came via Mexico and Texas, and by selective breeding by cattlemen on our great western plains, the commercially more desirable strain of the shorthorn became permanently dominant. In a way it seems regrettable that the rampaging old scraggly bovine scions of the glamorous days of the Spanish *conquistadors* had to succumb as they did in the great transition in the American West. But pawns as the species were in the hands of

"A Serious Predicament" –CHARLES M. RUSSELL–Courtesy I. B. Maytag

"Prospecting for Cattle Range—Wyoming"—FREDERIC REMINGTON

mercenary-minded men, it was that transition that brought vast amounts of wealth to the cattle industry on our western plains, and contributed in large measure to making our country the rich and powerful nation that it is today.

The cowboys who participated in the cattle drives from the Pacific Northwest, bringing shorthorns into Wyoming and other parts of the northern plains, had basically the same duties, problems, and, to a lesser degree, dangers as those driving the longhorns north from Texas. In fact, a good many of the men had begun their experience on those earlier drives. There were, however, some differences between driving shorthorns and longhorns. The shorthorns raised on the Oregon and Washington range were far from being as docile and tractable as were their barnyard brothers and sisters, although they were not nearly as wild and pugnacious as the early-day longhorns. Still, for the trail-driving cowboys, the unending days and nights in the saddle, through dust, rain, and wind, were much the same; and being scalped by a Sioux was not more pleasant to anticipate than the same at the hands of an Apache or Comanche. But there were some advantages: The pay was better, and the climate of the northern region was a blissful change. But no cowboy's life, no matter where he worked, was any bed of roses.

"Patch Hinton"—EDWARD BOREIN—Courtesy Dr. H. D. Burtness

Chapter 12

THE CATTLE BARONS

With their successful efforts in southeastern Wyoming, the cattlemen became determined to take advantage of the vast grass ranges of the North. The trail drives of longhorns from the South and shorthorns from the Pacific Northwest had poured so many cattle into the relatively small area that was safe for the new industry that new rangeland was needed. Moving herds into the North was restrained only by the fact the Indians were in possession of about two-thirds of the Wyoming Territory, and it was unsafe to take herds much beyond Fort Laramie. Furthermore, the federal government had designated a major portion of this northern region as Indian reservations and the rest as tribal hunting grounds; and the Indians were determined to use whatever means they chose to restrict the white men from encroaching into the region that rightfully belonged to them. And they had a special dislike to see the herds of the white men's cattle grazing on the grasslands where the all-important buffalo had once grazed and supplied the necessities of life for all the tribesmen for untold scores of generations. In fact, the treaty that had been signed in 1868 with Chief Red Cloud at Fort Laramie had literally barred cattlemen from operating in the whole northern part of the region that had become officially known as Wyoming Territory on July 25 of that year.

The cattlemen were well aware of the situation in the north. Even the remote Big Horn Basin had been investigated by the U. S. Cavalry under the guidance of Buffalo Bill Cody, who had decided that this mountain-surrounded region, flanked on the west by the majestic Rockies, would some day become the place where he would settle down on a ranch to spend the last years of his life. In the 1870s, however, it was no place for any white man to have a home, and least of all to raise cattle. The risks of taking cattle across the Big Horn Mountains were too great; and even if they were gotten into the Basin, the Indians might never permit them to survive. But these pioneer cattlemen were a rugged group of frontiersmen and were not to be discouraged or dissuaded in their determination. If it meant fighting Indians, they would fight Indians. Also, substantially organized as they were, the cattlemen had rapidly become a prestigious factor in the economic and political growth of the entire territory.

As more individuals became involved in the business of cattle raising in south-eastern Wyoming Territory, a group of these who were friends had decided to form an organization for their mutual protection against the possibility of Indian raids and to look after their mutual interests in the matters of raising and marketing their cattle. The industry was growing with great rapidity, and there were those who foresaw that it could spread over a million or more square miles of the freely available open range. There were but few local or federal regulations. The cattlemen had begun appropriating vast sections of rangeland, and ran things about as they chose—but some of them felt that an organization was needed to coordinate and protect their interests.

Because the young town of Cheyenne was conveniently located in the heart of the cattlemen's new domain, and was the center of population as well, it was selected as the capital of the territory and the administrative center for the cattlemen. Thus it was that a group of the leading cattle raisers of Laramie County met in the county clerk's office on November 29, 1873, and organized a *pro tem* association that they chose to call "The Laramie County Stock Association."

According to the records of the association, which were recorded and kept from the very beginning, those attending that first meeting selected M. V. Broughton as chairman and W. L. Kykendall as secretary. A committee was also appointed to draft suggested rules and regulations for a permanent association to be officially organized under the laws of the Territory of Wyoming. Another meeting was called and held on February 23 and 24, 1874, at which time twenty-five stockmen signed as members. The association became known as the Wyoming Stock Growers Association, and as such was properly established under territorial laws. This organization grew to be one of the most powerful in the history of the cattle industry—a virtual dictatorship in the territory and later the state of Wyoming.

There is no documentation to prove that members of the Wyoming Stock Growers Association exerted influence in bringing about the signing of the treaty of September

"A Wyoming Cattleman"–SKETCH BY EDWARD BOREIN

26, 1876, with the Sioux and northern Cheyenne Indians at the Red Cloud Agency in Nebraska. But this treaty did for the first time grant the cattlemen permission to use the vast rangeland that became the most important grazing area in Wyoming. In the light of influences later wielded by this same group, it is reasonable to assume that they had a great deal to do with this big step forward.

It was inevitable that these broad pasture lands, which had been the habitat of buffalo, antelope, elk, and deer and the often-contested hunting grounds of the Indian tribes, should soon see the introduction of cattle raising. There would be serious difficulties, first with the Indians and later with the equally inevitable spread of home-steaders. The treaties that had been made with the most important of the tribal chiefs were no guarantee that the Indian problems were ended. There were bands of roaming dissidents who at any time might choose to strike, without approval or reprimand from their tribal superiors. But this was nothing new for the Wyoming stockgrowers and the cowboys upon whom they depended to handle and protect their herds. They were accustomed to live in the shadow of Indian raids that endangered their cattle, horses, homes, and lives. The situation in northern Wyoming was different from any other region where cattle raising had been introduced, in that it was vastly greater in expanse and more distant from military protection. But with all the dangers, the cattlemen knew there was also that gold in the grass of every one of the virgin range-lands and that the harvest would belong to those who were the first to take control of the land and were strong enough to defend it against others who might covet it.

There was still another and quite different ominous black cloud gathering on the horizon, of which all the cattlemen and the Wyoming Stock Growers Association were aware. This was the obvious growing movement among certain representatives of both the federal and territorial governments to impose restraints and regulations on the free appropriation of the rangelands. It was believed that the Wyoming Stock Growers Association had become powerful enough to control the territorial represent-atives, but the federal government could be something else. However, the cattlemen were determined to take control of the new rangeland as promptly as possible.

Anticipating the northward movement of the cattle industry, the governor of Wyoming Territory made a tour of the contemplated areas in the summer of 1878. This included the Big Horn Basin. In Governor Hoyt's official report to the Secretary of the Interior for that year he stated that while he was in the Big Horn Country he "met several little parties of adventurous pioneers exploring for good locations with the intent of taking in herds of cattle the next spring."[27] And by the following year enough cattle and settlers had arrived in the newly created Johnson County, lying to the east of the Big Horn Mountains, to organize a county government.[28]

Not waiting for the Indian troubles to become completely controlled, and anxious to establish primary claim to areas of their choice, more cattlemen began traveling north. For some it was an independent venture; for others it was as representatives of groups of cattle raisers or of financial interests in the East or Europe. It was much like a gold stampede. There were some sizable parties, including cowboys rough and tough enough for anything that might arise. From the beginning the unwritten

"A Pronghorn Visits Camp"–FREDERIC REMINGTON

law was that the first one to effect squatter's rights enjoyed priority of claims, although realistically they had to be able to protect these rights against any outside force. Everyone was well armed; and there were undoubtedly some instances of drastic "claim jumping," the circumstances and eventualities of which were never made known, or conveniently blamed on an unfortunate attack by renegade Indians. This marked the beginning of rule of the cattle barons and the rather flexible code by which they operated. It also marked the beginning of a new breed of cowboys, whose duties extended considerably beyond that of handling cattle.

Each claimant to a cattle-raising range selected his own area, with a suitable location for the "home ranch" or headquarters, with boundaries established by natural geographic landmarks such as mountains, buttes, canyons, or streams. Available water was an important consideration, and the most desirable land in the area was chosen. Ranges thus claimed in some instances covered as much as five hundred to thirty-two hundred square miles. These claims, their locations, and boundaries were sometimes announced in a printed circular or newspaper; and this served as the equivalent of a deed, although there were at that time no land filings required by federal or territorial laws. The land was considered free for the taking, under the theory that it was public grazing land.

After the boundaries of a selected range were decided upon, the usual procedure was to build a headquarters in a desirable spot, preferably alongside a stream. The building was usually of logs and sufficient to accommodate a group of well-armed cowboys. Then all that was needed to be in business was to bring in a herd of cattle and have enough cowboys pugnacious enough in their extracurricular capabilities to protect the cattle and the boundaries of the newly established little feudal empire, to which each cowboy's unfailing allegiance was duteously committed.

In those early days of cattle raising on the northern prairies the majority of the cowboys were the hardened veterans of the longhorn drives from the South as well as the eastern movements of shorthorns from the Pacific Northwest. Some of the men had been raised in the mesquite country of southwestern Texas, and others were from Oklahoma or Kansas. They were a hardy breed of human beings, old hands at handling cattle. Most of them had at one time or more gone through the experience of having their outfit suddenly attacked by Indians.

It took a mighty good man to ride herd on a bunch of those early-day cowboys. The men who established and carried on the cattle-raising projects on the open ranges of northern Wyoming Territory had to have the idomitable pugnacity and courage that was necessary. The fact that those who survived and became prosperous came to be known as the "cattle barons" is very appropriate—and they earned that title. Most of these men were not new to the frontier, having previously been engaged in such things as fur trading, prospecting, overland freighting, and the like. Some had been raised on farms in Missouri or Ohio and been brought to the West as children in a family covered wagon. But they all had what it took to handle and dominate a bunch of pugnacious vassals and build for themselves little feudal cattle empires on the western frontier.

As the cattle raising prospered, it attracted more and more outside investment capital. Some of this was from the East, although a considerable amount was from Europe. This brought some personality changes, particularly among the cattle barons. Some of the old-time rough-and-rugged frontiersmen found that their nearest new neighbor, who might be something less than a hundred miles away, was a wealthy English titled aristocrat, a Scotsman whose father lived in a big castle, or a German with a title that no Wyoming cattleman could remember or even pronounce.

It is a bit surprising that so many wealthy and titled Europeans came to America

"The Dry Water Hole"–FREDERIC REMINGTON

"The Parley"–FREDERIC REMINGTON

for the express purpose of making an easy quick fortune. This was true even before the fabulous stories of the California gold fields were so widely circulated. And getting rich from raising big herds of cattle on the free grass of the wide open spaces of the great plains seems to have particularly appealed to Europeans who had plenty of money to invest. It certainly appeared as a more realistic business enterprise than searching for gold, or pursuing the example of a John Jacob Astor in trading for furs. There was also the added appeal of having a troop of cowboys do all the work, while they, the owners, might enjoy the excitements of hunting spectacular big game, and otherwise living a life of thrills in the wild and woolly American West. Some of these wealthy foreign fortune-seekers, who became a very sophisticated sort of cattle barons in Wyoming, formed exclusive little communities off by themselves and lived in a truly feudal fashion, even having polo fields for their private enjoyment.

There were other foreigners, though, who looked upon cattle raising in a truly serious manner. An example of this was a wealthy scion of German nobility by the name of Count Otto Franc von Liechtenstein. In 1878 he came into Wyoming's sequestered Big Horn Basin, where he established himself alongside the high snow-capped Rocky Mountains, not far from the present town of Cody, where the present writer makes his home. He became the first cattle baron of the region.

The Teutonic nobleman adopted an anglicized abbreviation of his name, and afterward until his death was simply known as Otto Franc. Having been raised in the mountainous region of southern Germany, the high, grassy prairies that extended back into the wide valleys that penetrated the majestic Absaroka Range of the Rockies adjacent to present Yellowstone National Park particularly appealed to the adventurous German aristocrat, and he established his home ranch near the headwaters of the Greybull River. The big log house that he built was about seven miles from a little stagecoach station, which was given the Indian name of Meeteetse. It was the nearest semblance of civilization, and that was two decades before the town was founded by Buffalo Bill Cody some forty miles' traveling distance to the north. Incidentally, the towns of Meeteetse and Cody later gained the reputation of being about the wildest and roughest frontier towns of northern plains; and the immediate region was one of the last to lose its wild frontier characteristics.

By 1881 Otto Franc's cattle empire extended clear across the Big Horn Basin to the Big Horn Mountains, a distance of about sixty miles to the east and an equal distance to the north, making an area of about thirty-six hundred square miles. He called his place the Pitchfork Ranch. This was his domain, and he ruled his range like the German nobleman that he was. He added his Old World ideas of intensive farming to the development of the land. Unlike most of the cattle barons, he spent a great deal of effort and money in draining and cultivating fertile sections adjacent to the Greybull River, where he raised hay and grain to supplement the vast open range and to provide emergency feed for the livestock when necessitated by severe winter weather. Otto Franc operated his cattle ranch on a profitable basis until 1903, when he was "accidentally killed through the careless handling of a shotgun." The Pitchfork Ranch is still in existence, although far from what it was back in the heyday of the Count Otto Franc von Liechtenstein.

The early 1880s were a boom era for the cattle industry on the open ranges of Wyoming. The national economic depression of the 1870s was over, and there was a rising tide of prosperity. Investment capital was still becoming increasingly available, and the industry had developed and prospered to the extent that promoters talked with glib assurances about the "beef bonanza" and the fantastic golden harvest of the cattle barons. Elaborate prospectuses were printed and circulated, offering investment interests in operating properties. One company, organized in Edinburgh, Scotland, in June 1882, offered participation in property in Wyoming "extending over an area of 4,000 square miles, of 2,560,000 acres of rangeland with 19,000 head of improved cattle, 150 saddle or work horses, dwellings and storehouses at the Home Ranch and branch establishments. . . ."[29] Other similar cattle companies were publicized as being capitalized at from 500,000 dollars to 3,000,000 dollars, with properties including 20,000 to 100,000 or more head of cattle. Ironically, however, in actuality in some instances the cattle had never really been counted, and for a few they never existed. These wildcat promotions were of course only a small part of the real situation, for according to the records of the Wyoming Stock Growers Association, "during the year 1883 twenty new companies, with a total capitalization of over twelve million dollars were incorporated under the Territorial Laws of Wyoming."

By 1885 the association's minute book records there were 400 members with 2,000,000 head of cattle, and that the total values of these were placed at 100,000,000 dollars. The association's executive committee had been enlarged to twenty-three members, representing a large part of Wyoming as well as sections of Nebraska, Dakota, and Montana; and association laws had been passed that in many ways created a virtual dictatorship over the ranges and the whole cattle industry. The entire area over which the association executed its influence was divided into thirty-three districts, over each of which a district chairman had full power to fix the time and place for the roundups and impose fines or penalties for violations of any of the rules established by the association. At the beginning the regulations were promulgated by the executive committee, although in 1884 the Stock Growers Association used its powerful influence to have these regulations passed as part of the Wyoming territorial laws. This dictatorial power contributed to the unfriendly and in some instances rebellious feeling against the big cattle barons by the little folks who were trying to establish themselves and raise families in the country.

To a considerable degree, prompted by the rising threat of the invasion of homesteaders (nesters) with their "damned barbed-wire fences," as well as sheep raisers with big flocks of woollies that nibbled away grass to the extent that a hardy shorthorn could starve to death on the same ground, the cattle barons and their Wyoming Stock Growers Association literally took over most of Wyoming, economically, politically, and otherwise. At the time, however, it seemed that the gold would never cease to continue flowing from the harvest of the roundups and the shipment of beeves to the eastern markets.

While the cowboys suffered the brunt of the hardships and difficulties of handling the big herds and driving them to the railroad shipment, there was a social side that was periodically enjoyed by the cattle barons that was an antithesis to their cowboys' life on the frontier open range. Attending the meetings of the Wyoming Stock Growers Association had its intermediate levities that went far beyond making new rules and regulations, or political intrigues.

The town of Cheyenne had become a very raucous and wide-open place. It was another Abilene or Dodge City, although for the cattlemen and a good many others who gathered there, the entertainment was largely on a rich man's plane of enjoyment. The association's meetings attracted all sorts of people, in addition to the regular members of the association. At all times the extraordinary Cheyenne Club was the center of both business and social activity. There were of course the big cattle owners; and in addition there were important representatives of the railroad, Chicago and Kansas City commission agents, bankers, potential investors or their representatives, and an occasional gate-crasher who was a disguised cardsharp or who had women to sell. "The Club" was a cosmopolitan place: reticent Britishers, cautious Scots, exuberant Irishmen, obstinate Germans, worldly New Yorkers, aristocratic Bostonians, chivalrous Southerners, and an occasional old-time frontiersman who was completely at home with any of them. Here men ate the best food west of the Mississippi River, drank generously the best whiskeys and wines, made deals involving big fortunes in cattle, gambled in games where the stakes were unlimited, boasted about the mistresses they had had, described their travels in foreign lands or the wars in which they had participated, played tennis, and watched horse races and bucking bronco exhibitions that were arranged for them. There has probably never been anything quite like it. This interesting life flowed along as though it would have no end, along with a feeling that the Cheyenne Club and the cattle barons' herds and the gold from their harvest would never cease to continue.

Chapter 13

THE NORTHERN PLAINS COWBOY

The cowboys on whom the cattle barons of the northern plains so completely depended for about everything except buying and selling and spending the profits, have become universally accepted as the classic American type. This in spite of the fact that they inherited from the Texas-Spanish originators of their profession virtually all the practices they followed, the gear they used, even the somewhat anglicized names and terms in their daily vocabulary. They all did much the same basic things in much the same way.

The differences between the early-day cowboys of the trail-driving era of the longhorns and the cowboys of the cattle-baron era on the northern plains were principally their family backgrounds and some variations in the garb they wore, such as style of hats and boots, and of course the warmer clothing required for winter weather. The northern cowboy was able to enjoy a far less nomadic existence than his earlier trail-driving counterparts and was able to develop a far stronger bond of fraternity among his own groups; and thus he developed closer friendships, had a higher regard for fair dealings, and generally had better relationships with his fellow workers. Each individual cattle range became a communal "home" for the men, and that also made a difference.

The home ranch on the northern plains was a well-established group of buildings, usually built of logs and situated among big cottonwoods near a stream of clear, cool mountain water. This was the center of operations and included a bunkhouse that was a home of sorts for the cowboys. This provided a nonnomadic atmosphere during the periods between roundups, trail drives to the railroad, and periodic line riding and checking on the herds. On the big spreads, whose range was too large to cover in a few days' riding, there were generally outlying camps that ranged from small sod-covered sleeping places, where most of the cooking was done over a fire built on the ground outside the low doorway, to sizable log buildings with bunks, plenty of blankets, grub, and sometimes even a camp cook during roundup and branding times.

No matter where the outfit's cowboys went, within the established boundaries of the spread, every cowboy considered the land his own and would protect it with his life. This was quite a contrast to that of being a trail-driving vagabond. Being a pawn of the cattle barons did not interefere in the strong pride they held in being a part of the whole project and the exclusive fraternity to which they belonged. The ranges on which they spent their days in the saddle were big and broad enough to satisfy the desire of any freedom-loving soul, and the life they lived was challenging enough to give them added pride in being its master, no matter how bitterly inclement the weather or difficult the situation might be. And, strangely enough, whenever they changed their employment from one ranch to another (which was not uncommon with those having a drifter's incentive), they generally transferred their allegiance at the same time.

One of the characteristics that the northern plains cowboy inherited from his Texas-Spanish predecessors was a haughty disdain for using his legs in the normal fashion of a biped, except when he stood with one foot on the foot-rail of a cowtown-saloon, or made an awkward attempt at participating in a very infrequent dance. And so far as walking into a saloon was concerned, he was known to sometimes ride his horse in through the swinging doors. He was so completely wed to a saddle on the deck of a spirited horse that he would rather waddle a hundred feet or more to get on his horse, just to ride the same distance to reach some unimportant objective.

If one might visit an old-time open-range cowcamp and observe a sizable group of the boys gathered around the chuckwagon campfire indulging in an evening meal, they might all appear as though they had come from the same neighborhood on the wrong side of the railroad tracks in the little town of Somewhere, U.S.A. And yet, of two apparent buddies sitting side by side cross-legged on the ground, each with a plate of grub on his lap, one might have been an honor graduate from an Ivy League university and the other a runaway dropout from the freshman class of a small-town high school. There were the sons of New England ministers and Georgia cotton farmers; those who maybe came from the richest families in town, to those who grew up in a county orphan home. They came from vastly different origins and for a good many personal reasons; but as cowboys they became all the same, molded into a closely knit class of men the likes of which had never been known. Probably because of the singular sort of life they led and the close fraternity that resulted, they developed certain ideas, ideals, and a sort of rustic philosophy that was peculiarly their own.

These men developed some very highly commendable principles that were respected and considered a part of their relationships among themselves as well as those regarded as outsiders. This code was stringently followed. Their rules of ethics were few and simple. A man's word was his bond and as binding. This, incidentally, was not restricted to the cowboys in those early days of the West, when a handshake was all that was needed to seal a bargain that could involve a small loan or many thousands of dollars or head of cattle. Another respected rule of relationship was fidelity of friendships. A friend should never be forsaken, especially in times of great need or

"Old-Time Cowboy–Pitchfork Ranch, Wyoming"–CHARLES J. BELDEN
PHOTOGRAPH

danger; and the double-cross was a cardinal sin in their unwritten book of unnumbered commandments. And while all of these riders of the open cattle ranges were invariably bachelors, their respect for women of good character was as strong a virtue as any man could possess. The open range was no place for a white woman. It was considered only "squaw country." On the infrequent occasions when a cowboy visited a cowtown for a bit of a holiday he was supposed to know the difference between the good and the bad; and one of the quickest ways to get into trouble was to make a pass at a woman who was married or known to be of good character.

The old-time cowboy was no western fashion plate. There were, however, certain accouterments with which he decorated himself that were considered indispensable to the well-outfitted cowboy. These were a rope that was conveniently tied to the saddle when not in hand; a six-shooter and cartridge belt, with a large knife in a scabbard; a vest with four pockets, in which to carry his sack of Bull Durham and brown cigarette papers, as well as some wooden or Chinese sulphur matches and maybe part of a plug of chewing tobacco; high-topped high-heeled boots; a pair of chaps (optional); a broad-brimmed hat; and a big neckerchief. As to putting on a fastidious appearance, he couldn't have cared less. What he wore in the way of traditional clothing was based on the most practical and essential needs of the season and the job at hand. His pants and shirts were preferably of substantial woolen material, for even during the sum-

"Leaving the Home Ranch for Roundup"–CHARLES J. BELDEN PHOTOGRAPH

mers on the northern plains the nights could be really chilly, and during the hottest days the woolen clothing absorbed the body sweat and was more comfortable. A cotton shirt could become just as smelly but would not withstand nearly as much wear and tear as heavy woolen material. The same was true of pants.

Not every cowboy wore a six-shooter at all times, although most owned one. The cartridge belt and gun were usually unstrapped and left hanging on the pommel of the saddle, or on a nail inside the door when a cowboy entered a cabin or ranch house as a visitor. This was normal etiquette. However, when going into a cowtown saloon, that was a different matter. When not strapped around the waist for possible use, cartridge belt and revolver were usually stashed away inside the cowboy's rolled-up bedroll.

The most highly prized luxury a cowboy knew was a pair of chaps. The word is an anglicized abbreviation of the original Spanish name, *chaparajos*. The use of these heavy leather leg protectors appears to have originated in Mexico or the early days in Texas. They were not absolutely essential to the cowboy in performing his normal duties. The chaps served as a protection to a rider's legs when chasing cattle through brush or thorn bushes; their weight made a long day in the saddle less fatiguing, by virtue of aiding the rider to keep his seat without muscular effort; they also added a bit of comfortable warmth when riding night herd or in a cold rain; and they played a big part in getting "dressed up" when making a visit to even the smallest cowtown. There were several varieties of chaps, fanciest of all being the "woolies" or Angoras, which became popular on the northern plains. The best were made of the skins of Angora goats, which had long and naturally curly and silky hair, sometimes dyed black, or brown, or even pink or blue. Occasionally a pair of the more common "shotgun" type of chaps was amateurishly covered with the hide of a bear or even that of a large long-haired dog. Any fur-covered chaps were especially desirable when riding out on the range when the temperature was a long way below zero and a ground blizzard was snorting down from the north country.

Probably the most indispensable item of gear the cowboy possessed was his "rope." The original Spanish name was *reata,* or *lazo* (lasso), and it was sometimes referred to as a lariat. For most cowboys it was unthinkable to go anywhere without their rope and the degree of skill with which the cowboy was able to use the rope was an important factor in establishing his qualifications as a cowboy in the estimation of the others with whom he worked. The rope or *reata* had always been something special, going back to the early days of the Spanish *vaqueros,* when the making of a fine *reata* was considered the work of a provincial master craftsman. The original *reata* was made from strands of rawhide taken from carefully selected hides of the longhorns, properly cut and cured, and braided by a real expert. The *reatas* were made in four, six, and eight strands depending of the special use for which they were intended. The four- and six-strand versions were made of smaller strands and were more pliable and intended for light work, while the eight was a heavy-duty product. The diameter of the finished *reata* varied, although the most popular was about three-quarters of an inch in size. After braiding was completed the *reata* had to be properly stretched, usually accomplished by tying one end to a tree and the other to the horn of a saddle on a quiet horse. This also served to test the strength and to even the tension.

In the early Spanish Colonial days, when longhorns were abundant and of small value, a *reata* maker would select a steer of proper age and condition, and kill the animal for his hide alone. Some of the real veterans in the business would only take a hide when the moon was in the right phase for doing so. Others preferred to use the hide of a steer that had died of hunger and been dead long enough for the hide to turn black, and had lost most of its fatty qualities (these supposedly made the strongest *reatas*

"Wyoming Roundup Camp"–CHARLES J. BELDEN PHOTOGRAPH

and required less tallowing in future use to keep them from drying out). The *reatas* were made in various lengths, ranging from thirty to as much as eighty feet. In some areas and among some *vaqueros* and cowboys there was a preference for the short lengths, to facilitate the quick dumping of a cow, although there were some who could make an accurate cast of fifty to sixty feet. On the northern plains most of the cowboys usually preferred to get close to the animal for roping, using the shorter length of rope. Even in the very early days, a fine *reata* was not a cheap article; and it was in California that use of the hemp rope first became popular. There the *vaqueros* learned that they could go into a store in any of the ports where the sea whalers bought their gear, and purchase a far less expensive length of "whaling rope" that served their own purpose almost as well as the same length of braided rawhide. Thus the using of the hemp rope began, although everywhere most of the old-timers preferred the traditionally made rawhide *reata*.

The northern plains cowboy used his rope for considerably more than just roping cattle. Like the California *vaqueros* who roped an occasional grizzly bear for a bear-and-bull fight at fiesta time, the Wyoming and Montana cowboys occasionally roped a bear just for the hell of it. In times of relaxation and just to have a bit of practice or fun, they would ride their horses at a fast clip going nowhere and try to rope each other; and in the later days, when there were little schoolhouses for the homesteaders' families, a new schoolmarm from the East was sometimes welcomed by the cowboys who went galloping through the schoolyard just to drop the flying noose around the startled miss when she was outside playing recess games with her young pupils. But the most common off-the-job use that the cowboy made of his rope was the continual practicing to perfect his skill. When the occasion was presented and did not interfere

"Shorthorns on Wyoming Open Range"–CHARLES J. BELDEN PHOTOGRAPH

"Roundup on the Musselshell" –CHARLES M. RUSSELL

"The Cowboy"—FREDERIC REMINGTON

"Roundup Chuck Time–Wyoming"–c. 1885

with work, he would try roping most anything, from a bunch of buffalo grass to a jackrabbit or a coyote.

The hats the cowboys wore showed more period and regional variations than anything else. They were invariably made of felt, although they ranged from the wide, floopy brims that predominated among the first Texas trail drivers, to later models that were of medium width with an inconsistent curl, and some that were flat and fairly stiff. The crowns of these hats were always large, although these changed from rather conservative size to the monster "ten-gallon" variety that first became popular in the Southwest and soon spread to the northern plains. They were creased or broken in different ways, to suit a local style or just a wearer's individual taste.

The cowboy boot as we know it today was developed during the period of the early cattle drives from Texas. It caught on quickly and became practically the universal footwear among cattlemen. Why the sharply pointed toes and the often uncomfortably tight fitting and the extraordinarily high, narrow heels are difficult to understand. The best explanation that has been given that the boot was designed to discourage all cowboys from ever learning to walk on the ground.

Most of the range riders smoked cigarettes. They always rolled their own, and the "makings" were the old reliable Bull Durham in a little white sack with yellow pullstrings and a round tag on the end. The desert-dry, finely cut tobacco was tightly rolled in brown rice straw paper, with amazing dexterity, even while riding at a gallop. The rolling of a cigarette could be done by some with the fingers of either hand, either toward the palm or outward toward the fingers, and there were some cowboys who could roll a cigarette with each hand at the same time.

Taking along a short-barreled carbine in a saddle scabbard was common practice at times when there was a probability of needing such a weapon. Involvement with hostile Indians, rustlers, or range wars always called for being fortified with more than a six-shooter. There were also times when an antelope, deer, or young elk was welcome as camp meat; and during the calving period it was always necessary to be on the lookout for predators such as wolves, mountain lions, or bears, which often persisted in infesting the range. Most cowboys were proficient in the use of both six-shooter and rifle. A favorite combination of weapons was a Colt revolver with a 7½-inch barrel that took the 44–40-caliber short ammunition, which could also be used in the Model 1873 Winchester rifle.

Long hair and a full beard were common among the early-day cattlemen. This was not in the spirit of Wild West extroversion, but the natural result of circumstances under which these men lived. Such things as a straight razor, a pair of scissors, or even a small mirror were not usually part of a cowboy's regular equipment. Sometimes the camp cook did a bit of hair clipping; but visiting a barber shop was one of the luxuries indulged in on the rare occasions when a cowboy went to town.

Also, because of circumstances and the life led by the early-day cowboy, he was not a habitual drinker. Liquor was a rare commodity on the cattle range. It did not set well on the top deck of a bucking bronco. Just as in the earlier days of the cattle drives north from Texas, the cowtown saloon and its associated attractions provided about the only holiday diversions and escape from the interminable grind of being in a saddle. Even under the nonnomadic life on the northern cattle ranches, such a thing

"A Skill Acquired from Long Practice"–CHARLES J. BELDEN PHOTOGRAPH

"Springtime on the High Prairies"–CHARLES J. BELDEN PHOTOGRAPH

as a regular vacation was unheard of. When a Wyoming cowboy did get to town, he went with a strong desire for things that had been deprived him through a long period of time. Just as in the days of Abilene and Dodge City, he went without inhibitions, and the gold coins in his buckskin poke were spilled out freely. Strong liquor was a stranger to him, and because of infrequent association, he was not accustomed to handling the new acquaintance. The result was obvious. But getting a bit drunk did not by any means establish his character any more than the rare occasion when he got bucked off his favorite horse indicated he did not know how to ride. No matter what he might have done when on a spree, the average early-day cowboy was a very normal, human sort of guy, and taken as a whole, he was far more good than bad. Any man with high respect for a chaste woman, and who would ride through the bitter cold of an untimely spring blizzard just to carry a little lost calf to a place of shelter, had to be a person with some real goodness in his makeup.

There were, of course, some downright bad characters who found their way into the frontier towns of the northern plains, and some of these gained employment in the cowcamps. It was a general practice to leave the door open to any stranger and to accept every man at face value until he proved himself undesirable. There were those who made good, and a few who became sufficiently unacceptable to be "dry gulched" some dark night or in a lonely place. As the cowboys sometimes put it: "They just got sent to sit on the edge of a cloud to learn how to play a harp." The attitude of most folks who learned about it, or helped in the burial at boothill, was a shrug and the quiet comment: "Too bad. But I guess he deserved it." In fact, it has always been

"Come Along Little Baldface!"–CHARLES J. BELDEN PHOTOGRAPH

boasted that there has never been a court conviction for murder in the Wyoming county of which the town of Cody is the county seat. But no convictions does not mean there have never been shootings; and all of those who contracted a fatal case of "lead poisoning" have generally been classified among those who deserved to become infected by that peculiar malady.

The cowcamp cook with the big outfits on the northern plains was every bit as cantankerous and extraordinary a character as any who ever cooked a meal over buffalo chips on a trail drive out of Texas. In fact, having a tradition to uphold, some of the northern Cookies were possibly an exaggeration of their predecessors. When the big, specially-built and -equipped later-day chuckwagon rolled out from the home ranch, pulled by four well-fed horses, its commissary included nearly everything in the way of food that could be purchased in the nearest general store. There was usually a favorite place to make camp, maybe in a cottonwood grove alongside a stream flowing with clear, cold mountain water; and maybe a grassy place suitable to put up a tent, in which the cowboys could bed down for the night. And when Cookie let down the chuckwagon endgate to form his working table, he had about everything any camp cook could think of to mix up to satisfy any bunch of hungry range riders. There was a relaxed atmosphere about the gatherings after the boys had finished the evening meal without any thought of having to move on the next morning, with all the problems of keeping a big herd of obstinate cattle traveling in an orderly fashion

"Branding Time"–CHARLES J. BELDEN PHOTOGRAPH

along a seemingly endless trail. The whole aura of those evenings was more condusive to singing their favorite old songs. The old-time cowboys were America's most extraordinary natural balladiers. It could hardly be classed as sweet music. Some of the tunes were drawn from memories of a boyhood church or Sunday school, although the words might be much too ribald for a cow to understand. The repertoire of these songs was surprisingly large.

The cowboy loved to sing, and he loved to tell or hear stories, and the taller or wilder they were the more he liked them. Every sizable cattle outfit had at least one story teller or camp jester who was always capable of relieving whatever monotony might arise when all the cowboys except the night herders were gathered around the campfire after the evening meal. Tall tales of the most outlandish imaginary proportions were the most highly regarded qualifications of a cowcamp story teller. This characteristic apparently originated during the Texas trail drives, for the cowboys of Texas origin are known to have been the best story tellers, and they delighted in fantastic exaggeration. In fact, some of those stories still survive, often with modification or changed background. A couple of the old favorites are worth repeating here:

"Down near Amarillo where I came from," said the cowboy from Texas, "my folks always hung a bell on me whenever I was out playing as a kid. They had to do it to keep the hawks from carrying us younguns away. Yes sir. My daddy once shot one of them Texas hawks that had a wingspread a little more than forty-nine feet."

"Jealousy"–CHARLES J. BELDEN PHOTOGRAPH

And, of course, the cowboy who came from down south of San Antonio retorted dryly: "Pshaw, pardner, down where I come from, we never usta shoot such young hawks as that."

Another old favorite and characteristic of the cowboys is the one about the traveling character who came into the cowtown driving a team of mountain lions hitched to his light buckboard, with a big old tom Texas wildcat sitting on the driver's seat alongside; and the visitor was using a big live Texas rattlesnake for a whip. This long-haired, big-bearded old character had two .50-caliber six-shooters and a big Bowie knife hanging from his belt. He stopped in front of the little cowtown store and asked one of the men who was standing there: "Where can a thirsty man get something to drink around here?"

When told the saloon across the road had a good variety of whiskey, the traveler let his live rattlesnake whip coil up on the seat to get a bit of rest, and shook his own hairy head as he chuckled: "Whiskey? Hell—that's no drink for a *man*, down where I come from. Ain't anybody round here got a bottle or two of sulphuric acid to sell a thirsty traveler?"

About that time the storekeeper had come to the door to have a look at the unusual traveler, and remarked that he just happened to have a bottle of sulphuric acid.

The traveler rubbed his hands with glee, and as the storekeeper went to get the bottle, the visitor dug out his poke to get the money. He drank down the whole bottle with loud gulps of gusto; smacked his lips; and thanked the witnesses for their kind hospitality. Then he picked up the rattlesnake, uncoiled him, and said, "Well, cats, let's get gowin'."

Before the mountain lions could get started, one of the local boys got enough breath to ask, "Stranger, where you from? We ain't seen the likes of you around here for some time." The reply was, "Oh, I'm from a little town down in Texas that nobody but me ever heard of." Before he could get started again the traveler was asked how come he left his home town, and the reply was, "Well, to tell the truth, they're runnin' all the sissies out'a my dear little town, an' I was the first one that had to leave."

Later on, when the little cowtowns had taken on more of the appearance of a real town and "tenderfeet" from the East began coming onto the scene, an old-time cowboy was occasionally asked how long he had been around that part of the country. These old-timers held tenderfeet in silent disdain; and the dry reply was apt to be,

"Forefooting a Mean One"–CHARLES J. BELDEN PHOTOGRAPH

"Well, stranger, its been a long time. See that mountain peak over yonder? Quite a sizable peak. Well, when I first came into this part of the country, that peak was just a prairie dog hole." Then afterward, as the old cowboy waddled on his way, he would probably grumble to himself, "Hell, that guy wouldn't have enough guts to make a sausage."

The cowboy's pay was always inappropriately small; and yet when winter came, most of them were laid off without pay to rusticate in their home ranch bunkhouse, or ride the grub line from one ranch to another, or rustle their own existence holed up in some dingy shack in some little cowtown with some congenial buddies asked to share the frugal existence until spring came again. However, they were always subject to recall at any time when a bunch of cowboys with a lot of guts were needed for any important reason. A few took winter jobs, as bartenders, cooks in little eating places, or at any other miscellaneous employment that might be found. Whatever it was or no matter how tough the times might be, however, there was seldom one who ever ceased to be a cowboy in heart and soul.

There was hardly a typical type by which to identify them. There were tall and skinny ones as well as short and robust ones, but they all had certain characteristics in common. One of their most distinctive attributes was their pungent, humorous,

"Cow Country Post Office–Big Horn Basin"–FREDERIC REMINGTON–Courtesy William Magee

"Riding the Barbed-wire Fence"–FREDERIC REMINGTON–James Graham Galleries, N.Y.

and often caustic vernacular; and they had a large vocabulary of profanity, which was seldom used in a vulgar or obnoxious manner. There was also a sentience of pathos, born of their dedication to a life in which having a wife and family were not compatible. In the later period when all things changed, however, a good many of them were compelled to abandon the life on the open range, and some married and settled down to enjoy the natural amenities of life; although many just retired to spend the remainder of their lives alone. The American cowboy of the northern plains was indeed a unique breed of man.

Chapter 14

CAUSES FOR CONFLICT

From its beginning the cattle industry in the American West had prospered largely because of the railroads. This was true when the first big herds of longhorns had come north to Abilene and Dodge City. In the late 1860s it had been the railroads that took the surplus cattle back to more civilized areas. It was also the same railroads that brought out onto the great plains the many thousands of homesteaders and builders of little towns who were continuing to bring about the great transition in the wilderness. It was these immigrants who had pushed the cattle raisers northward for what was to be their last stand on the open ranges.

Up in Wyoming and elsewhere on the northern plains and high prairies, the cattle ranges still seemed sufficiently remote and so well protected in a wilderness so inhospitable and infested with Indians determined to protect their native land from encroachment, that the cattle raisers believed they had found a land invulnerable to settlement by the homesteaders. The cattlemen had a derisive attitude toward the homesteaders.

However, the Wyoming cattlemen were aware of the effects that homesteaders had brought to other areas, and they realized that when the nesters began settling in any area it meant milk cows for the kids, chickens and pigs, gardens for the women, schools, churches, and whatnot. Then there would be roads, and barbed-wire fences across the open range and along the best streams, cutting off the best watering places for range cattle.

In spite of all this, the cattle barons optimistically tried to make themselves believe that in the seemingly remoteness of their free grass ranges the nesters with their plows and kids would starve to death or be killed by Indians. The land seemed undesirable for anything but cattle. But as the cattlemen were to learn, the railroads did bring the homesteaders to Wyoming and to all other parts of the northern plains, just as they had to other regions of the West; and wherever the railroads took the people, those people began moving out to find their own little piece of land on which to build a nest; and, if they wished and were able, they would put a barbed-wire fence around their section of land, which the federal government said they had the legal right to call their very own.

As time passed, and it passed very rapidly, it became quite obvious that the continuing transition from the old ways to the new was once again about to take place. This transition had a somewhat different impact upon both the cattle barons and the cowboys on the northern plains than on their counterparts in the more southern regions. It was not at all pleasant for the big cattlemen to even consider the possibility of anything jeopardizing their autocratic rule of the open ranges or their continuing to watch their big herds grazing upon the sprawling expanse of free grass and converting it into more and more gold for their personal coffers. For the cowboys, it had been a world over which a man could ride his horse in most any direction as far as a horse could carry him; and every step of the way that man could be thrilled with the feeling that this was his world and his alone. He could let his gaze drift out over the big grazing herd growing fat under the big sky by day; and when the stars came out at night, he could sing to them the crude lullabys he made up himself, while they both waited for another day to dawn. Being a cowboy was something very special, and he felt bound by a responsibility to defiantly protect his way of life against encroachment of any kind.

On the other hand, the nesters had their own creed, to which they were as strongly devoted as the most imperialistic cattle baron. Theirs was a creed of building homes and tilling the soil with the sweat of their own effort, and letting their family roots grow deep to nourish future generations; and all within the relatively small boundaries of their own barbed-wire fence.

In the days before the railroads, the homesteaders had come West in groups of ox-drawn covered wagons. The big wagons carried all the family's worldly possessions. They had to take along the family cow and generally a crate of chickens. The woman generally sat in the driver's seat and often held a baby in her lap. The wagon trains traveled hundreds of miles before each group reached a place where it was agreed they would each find their own spot to gamble on the future. Each family settled on its own isolated homestead, but the families were close enough to continue relationships with the other settlers and for protection against hostile Indians. These early pioneers were generally responsible for forming their own communities, and these were mostly established before the days of the cattlemen.

The later homesteaders to the remote regions of Wyoming and other parts of the northern plains came with the same desire of the earlier pioneers to establish themselves on their own small plot of land; but they did so under different circumstances. They came on the railroads instead of by wagon trains. Instead of being part of a group, they were largely loners. They invariably came to an established town, where they were able to purchase a wagon and team of horses, as well as the necessities in the way of food and tools with which to build a dwelling in which to temporarily live to till the soil for the beginning of permanent residence. They were prepared to face

"The Homesteaders"—W. H. D. KOERNER

the inevitable long, hard ordeal of toil and sorrow of making a future home for themselves and their future family on the land. These were the real little nesters that were the bane and derision of the big cattlemen; but they were destined to become the real nemesis of even the most powerful cattle barons.

Some of these loner homesteaders started out with practically nothing at all; and it is amazing how some of them survived and succeeded. There was even an occasional "good" woman who came alone on a train to find a husband and make a home and new life in the American West. Among these young unmarried women was one who came to Wyoming in the spring of 1882. Her name was Martha James. It was she whom Paul Frison knew as a neighbor; interviewed on numerous occasions until she was seventy-four years of age; and recounted her story in his locally published and historically important little book, *First White Woman in the Big Horn Basin.*[30] The beginning of that story is an excellent example of the courage and fortitude with which some of those pioneer homesteader women began their life in Wyoming. It is appropriate and worthy of being recounted here:

"Miss Martha James, a girl of twenty two, left her home in northern Wales, as Lady's Maid, to accompany the Right Honorable William Cairus Armstrong and his bride, on a trip to America, where they planned a honeymoon and visit with their friends in Cheyenne and at the 76 Ranch on Powder River, near Buffalo, Wyoming."

During the winter of 1882–83, while at the 76 Ranch, Martha James fell in love with one of the employees of the big ranch. "Frank Bull and I were married in May, 1883" she related. "If he had any idea I could not endure the worst that this country could force upon me, he was wrong. He had a place in mind where we could make a start with our new home. . . . Frank said there were trees, plenty of good water, worlds of grass and a rich carpet of flowers that covered the hills and valleys as far as one could see in every direction. . . . We left the ranch [where they had just been married], climbed into our wagon and set forth on the greatest adventure of my life.

As we turned the bend in the road, skirting the willows that lined the creek bank, I had Frank stop the horses and I stood up in the wagon my full four feet and eight inches, turned and waved a last farewell to some of the closest friends I had in the world. . . ."

After the first night of their journey: "As the sun came up over the horizon and cast its brilliant rays upon the Clear Creek bottom lands, it was to me the most beautiful sight I had ever witnessed. . . . Every foot of the way was alive with game animals. Deer and antelope, it seemed, were every place we looked. . . . We saw several bunches of elk, which was my first experience at seeing these animals.

"When we stopped for lunch that day, Frank gave me a big kiss and said: 'Martha, what would you prefer for lunch, trout, venison, elk, or wild grouse?'

"I replied, 'Are the grouse something like those back home?'

"In short order Frank had started a fire, killed and cooked two grouse . . . and we were soon continuing our journey. . . .

"We were three days arriving at the bend in the river where Frank had decided we would settle and build the log house we hoped would be the beginning of our own ranch. It was a beautiful spot, but Frank made me take a good look around, saying, 'Now Martha, if you don't like this place, say so and we can find one that suits you better.'

"I could not imagine any place that could be better, so we unhitched the horses, hobbled them and turned them out to graze while we began unloading things and getting ready for the night.

"We had not eaten our supper when ten or twelve Indians came riding down the creek. [It is probable they had been following and watching the intruders for some time.] I was frightened but Frank said they wouldn't hurt us . . . Frank jabbered with them for a short time while they apparently satisfied their curiosity, looking at everything we had. One tried to open my trunk, but it was locked. . . .

"I, the bride, had things to think of. Great dreams of the future! I was lulled into a happy world of fantasy. Drenched in this frontier fragrance and exquisite beauty . . . blue skies, song birds, pretty flowers, and this vast expanse of green grass. . . .

Only a couple of days had passed when "My dream was broken as a troop of soldiers appeared on the opposite side of Clear Creek. . . . The soldiers hollered across . . . to warn us that a white man had murdered an Indian girl and the Indians were acting as though they might go on the warpath. They told us we were taking a desperate chance if we did not leave at once. . . . So we decided to abandon our new home and start back to Buffalo at once. . . . We gathered up our few belongings and were soon on our way. . . .

"This sudden turn of events brought me face to face with reality. The beautiful landscape, the flowers, the song birds, the blue skies, and the sweet pungent odor from the sage brush were forgotten as we hurried as best we could. . . . [During the flight to safety they were compelled to cross the "creek," where it was deep and swift from the spring runoff from the snow in the high mountains; and during one crossing the wagon was swamped.] During this ordeal my trunk containing all my clothes and treasured items was lost in the river. . . .

"The evening of the third day following the departure, we arrived at Buffalo — thirty two days after Frank and I had left to begin life together."

The lot of Martha James Bull was a long and difficult one, with many disappointments and sorrows along the way. In spite of the fact that that first attempt at establishing a homestead ended in failure and frustration, she remained undaunted, to later participate as a wife and mother in the development of a modestly successful homestead, and she lived to a ripe old age in her adopted back country of the Wyoming frontier. The life and struggles of this brave woman are classic examples of the other side of the coin, representing the nesters and the fulfillment of that quiet but irrefutable juggernaut that became the nemesis of not only the cattle barons and the great herds, but also the era of the old-time cowboy.

The nesters were not the only local annoyances and causes for conflict on the part of the big cattle outfits. Cattle rustling greatly increased in direct proportion to the outside population that was steadily coming into the region; and horse stealing was on an upward trend because of the ready market among the newcomers being continuously brought into Wyoming on every railroad train that arrived from the East. There was also the threat of sheep men bringing in flocks that could nibble a range so clean of grass that the jackrabbits couldn't find a square meal.

The plans of the nesters and the sheep herders were obvious to the cattlemen, although cattle rustling and horse stealing were always carried on with carefully planned secrecy and subterfuge, which made apprehension and punishment difficult or sometimes impossible. In case a nester should camp on one of the ranges with apparent

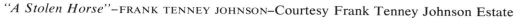

"A Stolen Horse"—FRANK TENNEY JOHNSON—Courtesy Frank Tenney Johnson Estate

intentions of becoming a settler, several cowboys, all wearing six-shooters or with rifles in hand, would pay the intruder an unfriendly visit, and in the strong vernacular of which they had a large assortment: "What'n hell you doin' here on our range? We don't like neighbors—and sometimes we have to get right rough to get rid of 'em. Now let's stay sorta distant friends. Understand? We'll be back about this time tomorrow —an' if you know what's good for you, you damn well better not be here. This is a big country. Understand?" It was a big country; and the nester usually moved on.

The rustler problem was the result of the large number of mavericks that were to be found on the ranges, especially those that included a considerable amount of rough country, which abounded in most parts of Wyoming. Webster defines a maverick as "an unbranded range animal, especially a motherless calf." The dictionary also gives a second meaning: "an independent individual who refuses to conform to his group." To the cattlemen it strictly meant unbranded cattle; and the name and the problem it represented were a lot older than Webster's Dictionary. There are a number of stories of the origin of the term. They involve a Texas cattleman who had a large longhorn ranch about forty miles south of San Antonio. His name was Col. Samuel Maverick; and one of the presumably authentic stories is that in the mid 1840s the black slaves the colonel had on his big ranch were too lazy to brand his cattle, and these thus became known as "Maverick's cattle." The other stories all involve un-branded cattle, some of which the colonel may have appropriated for himself, or ones that other people took for their own. Whatever the true story might be, unbranded range cattle came to be known as mavericks. The men who trail-drove those long-horns north carried these ideas with them; and thus the accepted custom regarding mavericks was preserved.

In the early days of the open ranges some of the cowboys were sent out by the

"The Cinch Ring"—CHARLES M. RUSSELL

"Through the Starlit Hours"–FRANK TENNEY JOHNSON–Harold McCracken Collection

"Prairie Sun"–W. H. D. KOERNER

"Half-breed Horse Thieves"–FREDERIC REMINGTON

big cattle owners to "rustle a few mavericks" that no one had branded. The employer's brand was put on these animals. The cowboys sometimes received extra remuneration for their efforts. The freshly branded mavericks may have rightfully belonged to the same outfit, or maybe they did not. The rule of the range was that any unbranded stock was anybody's fair game; just as any branded stock was the property of the owner of the brand it carried, no matter where that animal might go. During the winters, when the cattle were left pretty much to shift for themselves, it was only natural that some cattle would on occasion wander considerable distances and become mixed with drifters from other herds. It was the purpose of the spring roundup to search for, find and separate the cattle according to the brands they wore; and it was the whole basic purpose of branding cattle and having the brands properly registered. However, on the expansive ranges that included such a large amount of really rough and rugged country, it was only natural that a large number of cattle would find their way into places where they would remain unbranded, unclaimed, and free game for whomever might find them.

This inaugurated the practice of paying a cowboy a couple of dollars a head whenever he brought in unbranded cattle that happened to be missed in the regular roundups, no matter where he happened to find them. The extra pay inspired some cowboys to go beyond their own ranges to pick up strays. It was perfectly legitimate. But it gave the idea to other folks to make a business of surreptitiously seeking out (or "rustling up") unbranded cattle wherever and on whomsoever's range they might be found, and selling the meat and hides, or in this way starting a little herd of their own. As more and more immigrants and itinerants began coming into the back country regions, the number of these maverick hunters increased; and they came to be known as "rustlers." Some of the more unscrupulous even found that it was not too difficult to make some changes on most of the brand marks that were used. This could be accomplished with nothing more than a round iron ring, commonly used as part of every saddle equipment and known as a "cinch ring." Easily heated to a red-hot temperature over a small fire, this cinch ring, sometimes referred to as a "running iron," could be easily manipulated to alter existing brands. Some individuals began making quite a profitable practice of this and became expert in reburning most any brand to suit themselves, for adding to their own illegitimate herd. These became the real rustlers, who became another serious bane of all cattlemen. The ranchers and cowboys made a practice of hunting down the rustlers as they would predatory animals. Some were tracked down and hung from a limb of the nearest cottonwood tree. The same was true of those who made a practice of stealing horses. Thus a practice that orginally was part of the accepted unwritten law of the cattle country became something disdained in the face of established law and justice—although even this was to take a rather ironic change in public opinion, which was to reach a climax in the famous Wyoming Johnson County War.

The Wyoming Stock Growers Association made a diligent effort to settle the maverick and cattle-rustling problems. They used their influence to have a Wyoming territorial law passed 'defining a real maverick, and stipulating that all such were to be considered property of the Association . . . branded with an 'M,' the official brand of the Wyoming Stock Growers Association." The foreman of every roundup district was to be instructed by the law to take up all mavericks found and offer them for sale at auction on the range every ten days, while the roundup was in progress; and in the presence of the association's foreman, the purchaser was to be required to place his own brand on the animals. The money from the sales was to go into the treasury of the association for payment of brand inspectors and "for other purposes."

As more and more nesters and town builders established themselves, a feeling of resentment and jealousy developed against the big cattlemen and their imperious monopoly of such vast areas of grazing land. It was known that they held no legal rights to the land on which their herds of cattle grazed, and that they were growing rich on its free use. This feeling was growing particularly antagonistic against the eastern and European capitalists who were operating in Johnson and Natrona counties, just east and south of the Big Horn Mountains, although the feeling extended over a wide area. This attitude on the part of the nesters, small-town folks, and particularly those who were struggling to develop small herds of cattle, provided a growing incentive to cattle rustlers. Even some of the honest small-fry ranchers began seeking unbranded cattle to add to their little herds.

The cattle industry spread rapidly up into Montana and Dakota. In Montana there were great areas of tableland prairie with considerably less rugged mountainous areas than in Wyoming. Cattle rustling and horse stealing greatly increased everywhere, especially in Montana. There were some areas where the rustlers who were taking beef cattle or calves for one reason or another actually outnumbered the big cattlemen and all their cowboys. The country was rapidly becoming populated, and there developed a strong sympathetic attitude toward the rustlers as being some sort of western Robin Hoods challenging the wealthy cattle barons; and when the local agencies of law and order and courts of justice were established in the outlying regions, it became very difficult if not impossible for any of the big cattlemen to obtain a conviction in court against even the most flagrant rustler or horse thief.

The cattlemen were compelled to band together and organize vigilante committees to protect themselves against the growing outlawry and the widespread prejudice against them. Taking the law into their own hands only aggravated the whole situation, although it did to some degree decrease the depredations being practiced. The vigilantes in most instances tried to be fair in meting out their exceedingly drastic penalties. In many cases they gave warnings to the strongly suspected rustlers to get out of the country in a specified limited length of time, or suffer the consequences. After further due course of consideration by the vigilantes, they summarily shot or hanged the convicted suspects the next time they were found. This was more characteristic of the situation in Montana than in Wyoming. It has been substantially claimed that in one intensive campaign in Montana, "the vigilantes killed between sixty and eighty of the rustlers; and one railroad bridge on one morning had thirteen corpses swinging from it."[31]

However, in spite of the numerous hangings by vigilantes and independent cattlemen, the tide of antagonism against the cattle barons was difficult if not impossible to turn. Rustling continued to increase, as did the nesters and the towns where the increasing number of sympathizers with the "Robin Hood" rustlers became more inclined to buy their beef without asking questions as to how the meat was obtained. Once again, time, circumstances, and the space for free open range for the great herds were running out. The juggernaut of inescapable change was rolling steadily on, toward a dramatic climax.

"Cowboys with a Past" — NICK EGGENHOFER

"The Rescue"—CHARLES J. BELDEN PHOTOGRAPH

Chapter 15

WHITE CATASTROPHE

Through all the trials and tribulations created by dealings with homesteaders, mavericks, rustlers, and horse thieves, plus the normal problems of handling big herds of cattle on the open range, roundups, and driving the beef cattle to the railroad, it was always the cowboys who were called upon the take care of the situation. They had not particularly minded fighting the rustlers, for the hard core of those who perpetrated the premeditated deeds of thievery against the cattle industry were operating on a principle that was contrary to the accepted code of most of the cowboys, and the cowboys considered it an affront to themselves and their profession. Furthermore, among the most active of the cattle rustlers and horse thieves were some of the roughest, toughest, and most dastardly men who ever rode the range in a saddle. Their whole purpose was based on plans to outsmart the most expert of the legitimate old-time cowboys; and this added considerable zest and determination to apprehend the rustlers and eliminate them from the scene.

The cowboys of most every big outfit, during the decade of about 1876 to 1886, had constituted impromptu and unofficial vigilante committees of their own; and when a rustler of cattle or horses was apprehended on their range, he was generally shot on the spot. On the other hand, dealing with the nesters was a little different matter to most cowboys. But they were like good soldiers, and on the orders from their high superiors some nesters were regretfully shot.

Of all the physical displeasures that affected the cowboys' life, the weather could be the most unpleasant. Although they became accustomed and almost impervious to long days, nights, and weeks of physical fatigue, there were periods of blistering summer heat and subzero blizzards in winter that were extremely difficult for any human being to take. And the worst ordeal of this kind in the whole story of the American cowboy and the history of the cattle industry on the western plains was the awful winter of 1886–87. This followed on the heels of a summer that was almost as bad in its own way. Ironically, this came at a time when the cattle industry on the entire northern plains had risen to an all-time peak of prosperity. According to records in the Montana Historical Society Library, the relatively small Judith Basin spring roundup amounted to twenty-five thousand head; and the Flat Willow pool was a record fifty-six thousand. This was typical of other roundups held in similar areas throughout Montana, Wyoming, western Nebraska, and Dakota. The summer that followed quickly on the heels of that delightful spring period of roundups, however, brought a widespread, devastating drought. The intense heat and almost total absence of rain turned the great expanses of free grass pastures into a virtually blistered desertland. The streams and waterholes dried up. The parched grass was not only unfit for the proper fattening of market beef, but a great many animals died, and those that survived were sadly undernourished. The dry grass also made tinder for numerous prairie fires, which destroyed large areas of the cattle ranges. Thousands of cattle perished in the smoke and flames. It was rumored that vengeful Indians were responsible for starting a good many of the fires, and whether this was true or false did not relieve the widespread harm that was done. In many areas the cattle became walking skeletons. Everywhere the cowboys struggled to do whatever they could. Some small herds were driven back into valleys in the mountains where grass and water were somewhat more available; but on the whole, the cowboys' efforts were largely in vain to avert the calamity; and only the coyotes, wolves, mountain lions, and magpies got fat during that extraordinarily hot summer of 1886.

Then came a winter that is recorded as the worst in the history of the West. The stock were in no condition to withstand even a reasonably cold winter. Practically all of the cattle raisers had through the previous years depended upon the free grass of the open range for the sustenance and fattening of their big herds, and virtually none had raised hay for emergency rations. Most of the cowboys were kept on the job from the beginning of the unusually early coming of the bad weather, although there was little assistance anyone could render. Winter came with a merciless blast.

Quoting from the record, under date of November 17, 1886, the Chicago News Service sent out the following summary of the situation as reported by the United States Signal Corps office: "*Omaha:* It has been blowing a blizzard since early this morning and every railroad is more or less blocked. Travel is entirely suspended. The storm is general throughout the plains region. . . . *Sioux City:* A train with one hundred passengers on board is snow-bound eleven miles west of Canton, Dakota. . . . *Denver:* The west bound Kansas Pacific mail train has been snow-bound at Brookville since Monday. The east bound train, delayed at Hugo, is expected through tomorrow. No Burlington train (from Billings, Montana, through Wyoming) has arrived since yesterday. . . . *Sioux Falls:* More snow has already fallen than during the entire of last winter. . . ." And this was only the beginning. Along with the never-ending blast of the Arctic wind sweeping down across the whole northern plains, the temperature slipped far below zero and remained there. The temperature was much lower throughout the high prairies, where the conditions were far worse. In the rough country the deep snow drifted and filled every ravine, making death traps for the thousands of cattle that instinctively drifted before the storm. Many of the stock raisers faced complete ruin before the winter had hardly begun.

"Drifting Before the Storm"–FREDERIC REMINGTON

The cowboys were called on as they never had been before. True to their trust, they rode out into the blizzards to make valiant efforts to herd remnants of scattered herds into places of comparative shelter or into places where a little natural feed might be found; or to keep the emaciated stock moving rather than just standing to be frozen to death in their tracks. There was scant shelter, if any, for man or beast. Riding all day in the saddle became agony almost beyond endurance for even the most rugged man, whipped as they were by the icy lashes of the storm and stung to the bone by the freezing cold. A considerable number of cowboys failed to return to the bunk-house, and their bodies were often not found until the snow melted the following spring. Many of those who returned came in with frozen faces, hands, and feet.

The bad weather was interminable. There were no breaks to give at least temporary relief; many prayed for a warm "Chinook" wind from the west to push aside the Arctic wind and cause the temperature to rise and melt the snow on the ridges, where some dead grass might be found to save cattle as well as wild game from starvation. Even the freight wagons could not get through to isolated small communities, where there was a serious shortage of food and kerosene for human needs. On February 2, 1887, according to the *River Press,* the little local newspaper at Fort Benton, Montana, the temperature was 42 degrees below zero and the gale still blowing from the north. There was a footnote added at the end of the report: "The result will be immense losses in stock . . . cattle are dying by the wholesale."

It was not until March 2 that the arrival of a desperately awaited warm Chinook wind was reported by the *River Press:* "The Chinook which has been blowing . . .

with the temperature going up to 42 degrees above zero and the warm wind attaining an estimated velocity of 30 to 50 miles an hour, has rapidly melted the snow. But it has been tardy in coming. . . ." Then a week later the little newspaper reported: "Our losses in cattle are simply immense. . . ." The same report could appropriately have been made from most other areas of the northern plains.

It was not until the snow had melted the following spring that even the cowboys who had been out on the range learned the full extent of the disaster. Dead cattle were found everywhere, particularly in the ravines, where they became trapped in such deep snow that they did not have the strength to get out. Many of the emaciated remnants of the once-great herds that had managed to survive, hobbled about on the results of badly frozen feet; legs and ears were also frozen, and the cattle were so weak they could barely move about. Over large areas of Montana, Wyoming, and Dakota, the results of that winter of 1886–87 were estimated in losses as high as 75 percent to 90 percent of the cattle owned by some of the large outfits. For a good many of the formerly prosperous cattlemen, their herds were completely wiped out.

According to John Clay, who was as close to the situation as anyone: "At the 1887 Annual Meeting (of the Wyoming Stock Growers Association), held on April 4 . . . neither the President, Vice President nor Secretary was present . . . After this they began to disintegrate. . . . The old love of the open range, the burning fires of desire of the old days were smothered . . . and the old regime passed away."[32]

"*Last of the* 5,000–CHARLES M. RUSSELL–Montana Historical Society

This is the real thing painted the winter of 1886 at the OH ranch
C M Russell

This picture is Chas. Russell's reply to my inquiry as to the condition of my cattle in 1886. L E Kaufman

"Sheep on Wyoming Hills"–CHARLES J. BELDEN PHOTOGRAPH

There was one Montana cowboy, however, for whom that bitter winter proved to be a blessing in disguise. During the whole ordeal he had been working for one of the cattle outfits in the Judith Basin of central Montana, with another cowman by the name of Jesse Phelps, who had been detailed to look after the cattle belonging to the Kaufman and Stadler combine, whose headquarters was in Helena. Phelps' aide in the work was Charles M. Russell, who had been in Montana six years, spending nearly all of that time working as a cowboy in the Judith Basin, and having gained a bit of a cow camp reputation as an amateur artist. By his own admission he wasn't much of a cowboy. Along toward the end of the winter a letter was received from Kaufman, asking for a report on the situation regarding the herd, which had numbered about five thousand head. Jesse Phelps made an attempt to write a letter breaking the sad news, but he did not have the heart to tell Kaufman the whole truth. He asked "Kid" Russell for help, and finally finding a piece of paper about two by four inches in size, Russell got out his watercolors, which were carried around in an old wool

"End of a Bitter Winter"–NORM HILL PHOTOGRAPH, Billings *Gazette*

sock, and sketched a starved-looking cow wearing the Kaufman-Stadler brand on its bony flank and humped over in the snow ready to keel over, while some hungry coyotes waited to begin the meal that seemed soon to be theirs. This they put in an envelope and mailed to Kaufman with only the added notation in lieu of a report: "Waiting for a Chinook."

When the little watercolor was received at the Kaufman and Stadler office in Helena it created quite an impression. It conveyed the message, more impressively than a thousand-word report might have done, as to what had happened to the five thousand head of cattle. Kaufman titled it "Last of the 5,000," showed the picture around town, and it became famous throughout the Montana cattle country. Postcards were made of the little picture, which were widely distributed; and it no doubt did more than anything else to give Charles M. Russell the beginning for his rise to fame as one of the greatest of America's western artists. He was probably the only person involved in the cattle business for whom that disastrous winter led to lasting good fortune.

Chapter 16

CLIMAX IN VIOLENCE

The cattlemen and the whole cattle-raising industry suffered their greatest catastrophe that bitter winter of 1886–87. It had devastated many of the big outfits. Many of the absentee eastern and European financiers, who had been in the business only for the profits to be gained, made no attempt to reorganize their holdings, but took the losses and got out as best they could. Some of the scions of wealthy and titled foreign aristocratic families stayed in the cattle business with what was left of their herds and continued to enjoy the frontier luxuries of their big ranch houses, riding behind their packs of hounds, hunting big game, and having an occasional game of polo. And there were others, and a goodly number they were, indomitable cattlemen of the old school, who refused to be stopped by severe adversity. These were determined to go on; and they chose to do so in the face of a strong rising tide against the cattle industry being carried on in the old way. Many of the constraining influences were obvious. The number of homesteaders and townspeople was increasing at a rapid rate, and barbed-wire fences were spreading out over the country like an epidemic. Sheepherding was increasing. An ever-increasingly antagonistic feeling had been developing against the big cattle outfits operating on the open range, along with the sympathetic attitude toward the lawless practices of mavericking unbranded calves and cattle.

Popular sentiment against the big cattle outfits had become so strong in some places that it was next to impossible to get a town jury conviction against any cattle rustler, no matter how strong the evidence might be against the defendant. This was particularly true in Johnson County, in the Big Horn country of northern Wyoming. In some cases of cattle rustling and other illegal practices against the big cattle outfits, county law enforcement had virtually broken down.[33]

The catastrophe of 1886–87 had taught the cattlemen that the great herds on the free grasslands were intolerable risks, without being able to provide sufficient emergency feeding. The development of the necessary amounts of land for the raising of an adequate supply of hay for another such winter seemed to be a practicable and economic impossibility. This meant smaller herds. But still there were men who were determined to go on as they had in the past.

One of the frailties of human nature is the tendency toward conflict on the part of the have-nots against those who have much more. There was of course much to justify antagonism against the wealthy cattle barons, particularly the foreigners and the absentee owners who visited their ranches only occasionally to hunt big game. In the small-town general stores and nearly everywhere the local folks gathered, the big cattlemen were a popular topic of conversation, and there was no doubt a considerable amount of exaggeration in the stories that went the rounds. These would naturally include the amounts of gold that all of the owners of the big outfits had been making; the exclusive parties that were being enjoyed in luxurious big ranch houses; and the fancy women riding side-saddle and wearing long black skirts when they went along to follow the packs of hounds that were imported just to chase coyotes and wolves. When some of the cowboys came to town they must have created and given credence to some of the stories. A couple or more of the cowboys were generally taken along on the hunts with the hounds, just to serve as bodyguards for the women and to skin a captured quarry if any of the riders should indicate a desire for the hide. For a cowboy to tell about such as this could be innocent chitchat, although added to the many other imagined or true stories it all added up to strong resentment, which easily became magnified into serious bitterness.

"Wyoming Cattle Roundup"–c. 1891

"Wyoming Trail Herd"–JACK RICHARD PHOTOGRAPH

After the winter of 1886–87 the big cattle outfits were not as powerful or as well organized as before, and the cattle rustling increased dramatically. In most areas the cattlemen retaliated by intensifying the activities of their vigilante committees, hiring range detectives, and in some instances they hired gunmen to kill rustlers of established reputations. Wrongdoing was committed by both sides, to the extent of serious disregard for the law. One reported thief who had a well-known reputation of never having owned a cow by acquiring it honestly, drove to market a herd of yearlings of the same age and size equal to the offspring of the largest herd in the area; yet no one challenged him.

When Wyoming was admitted to the Union on July 10, 1890, a good many of the ordinary residents of the former territory assumed they had been granted a special franchise to prey upon the big cattlemen with wanton abandon. This only resulted in more reprisals, hangings, and shootings by the cattlemen. Step by step it all led to one of the most notorious, if not the most sanguine, of all the range wars in the history of the cattle industry. Just a few of the progressive incidents that culminated in the "Johnson County War" of 1892 are given here. They are characteristic of a good many other similar happenings that led to bloody violence.

On a night in July 1889 a posse of Wyoming Carbon County ranchers hanged a man and woman from the same tree in what was locally known as Spring Creek Gulch

"Dust-stained Riders"–FRANK TENNEY JOHNSON–Courtesy Frank Tenney Johnson Estate

on the Sweetwater, not far from Independence Rock, the famous landmark on the Oregon Trail. The two hanged persons were widely known as Jim Averill and "Cattle Kate." Averill ran a little store on Horse Creek, where whiskey was his main stock-in-trade. Ella "Cattle Kate" Watson Maxwell, sometimes known as Kate Averill, was a buxom, good-looking gal, who sold herself with no questions asked whenever a local or passerby had the required payment of a calf or two. She and Averill acquired quite a herd, and it was well known that they did not all come from Kate's involvements with other men. Averill openly admitted that he hated every one of the big ranchers in the area, and he wrote letters to the newspapers denouncing them as tyrants and land-grabbers, and made other accusations unfit to print. Obviously fed up with the barrage of the reformer's invectives, a small posse came one night and took the unsavory pair to Spring Creek Gulch and hanged them from the same big cottonwood tree. Six ranchers were arrested as lynchers, although they were never brought to trial.

On the afternoon of November 30, 1891, a thirty-nine-year-old Johnson County rancher by the name of John A. Tisdale was driving home from the town of Buffalo with a load of supplies. It was said that Tisdale was once foreman on Theodore Roosevelt's Elkhorn Ranch in North Dakota and had a good reputation in Johnson County. As he was driving by Haywood's Gulch about eight miles south of Buffalo, he was shot from ambush. His body was found by a neighbor who happened to be riding along the road and was close enough to hear the shots. When the news reached Buffalo, Sheriff W. H. (Red) Angus hurried with a posse to the scene and found John Tisdale dead, among the Christmas presents he was taking home for his wife and three children. The accepted explanation was that Tisdale had been accused of mavericking on one or more of the big ranches, and had been shot by a hired gunman.

With such high-handed actions as this, whether true or false, a bitter and intensive confrontation was inevitable, and it came just east of the Big Horn Mountains, in Wyoming's Johnson County, where tempers were running the hottest on both sides. Much has been written about the Johnson County War (sometimes also called the "Cattlemen's invasion of Wyoming") of 1892. In the beginning the facts are quite clear, although the whole story became, and in Wyoming still is, as controversial as the Custer Battle on the Little Big Horn, which occurred only a short distance to the north.

On the morning of April 5, 1892, a special train from Denver arrived in Cheyenne.

"Fight for the Water Hole"–FREDERIC REMINGTON–Courtesy Frank Tenney Johnson Estate

There was one passenger coach, with the blinds pulled down, and inside were twenty-five men who had been brought into the state as hired gunmen by important cattle interests. The gunmen were mostly from Texas and were selected for their reputations in handling violent situations. There was a baggage car and flat car carrying camp equipment and other gear as well as supply wagons. There were also three stock cars carrying horses. At Cheyenne the traveling group was joined by an additional twenty-five men, mostly ranchers, ranch foremen, stock detectives, and other interested parties. The special train left immediately for Casper, where the entire entourage disembarked, and the cavalcade headed for Johnson County.

What happened from the time the invaders arrived at the scene of their intended action, until its unanticipated ending, has been the subject of disputed intentions, involvements, and interpretations, all hotly contested in the post-mortems by both sides. The first book giving a detailed on-the-spot account of the conflict was *The Banditti of the Plains*, privately printed in February 1894, by Asa Shin Mercer,[34] a competent and reputable resident of the town of Buffalo, which was the county seat and center of the Johnson County War. The book made such serious accusations against the cattlemen and their political involvements, going into some of the highest offices in the state, that a very intensive effort was made to seize and destroy every copy.

It is not my purpose to take sides in a matter that can still raise a heated controversy in the region where I make my home. However, it is hardly beyond doubt or dispute that the cattlemen did make a premeditated invasion into Johnson County and that they brought with them a large group of hired mercenaries. Their purpose was to eliminate a class of people whom they accused of stealing their stock. In this work they proposed to "kill without hesitation, with ordinary weapons of warfare, and to destroy all ranch houses in the country." That the carrying out of the invasion supports such an intent is pretty well substantiated by the facts. Furthermore, just as General Custer misjudged the strength and intensity of his opposition, so did the cattlemen err in their attempts to "cleanse" Johnson County.

The Johnson County War drew widespread attention because of its sensational aspects, the repercussions that shook the very foundations of the important cattle-raising industry, and the political implications that carried as far as the United States Congress and the White House. This prompted the writing of a large number of newspaper and magazine articles, and inclusion at some length in a good many books. These include nationally recognized writers. It was the sort of story that was easy to influence a prejudiced opinion in favor of one side or the other, or to be unintentionally or deliberately inaccurate or deceptive. Furthermore, both sides put forth stringent efforts to have their own case presented as widely as possible.

Probably the most forthright and realistic attempt to present the facts in an unprejudiced manner was the account assembled and presented in the April 24, 1892, issue of the Buffalo *Bulletin,* a weekly newspaper. The previous issue failed to be published because the head printer was out on duty with the local militia, endeavoring to establish law and order between the warring factions. The report was printed the

"Hard Winter"—W. H. D. KOERNER

"After the Dance"–NICK EGGENHOFER–Courtesy Miss Lori Goppert

week following the end of the conflict, when all the facts were freshly assembled. Some of the statements aroused the bitter ire of both sides and resulted in a prompt raid on the newspaper's printing establishment, and what was believed to be the entire issue of an estimated one thousand was confiscated and destroyed. At least one copy is presumed to have survived. Unfortunately, for sixty-three years that firsthand report of the facts was lost to the permanent record. It was not until 1955 that the *Bulletin's report made its reappearance by being reproduced in a limited edition of one thousand facsimile copies;*[35] and it is from one of these that the following on the Johnson County War have been taken.

The editor of the Buffalo *Bulletin* prefaced the report with this statement: "The

"Land Beyond the Law"—FRANK TENNEY JOHNSON

people of Johnson County . . . were suddenly awakened from peaceful pursuit . . . by the events of last week. It is the aim of this paper to give in these columns an unbiased account of the week's happenings."

The *Bulletin's* report then continues: "On the night of April 6 there arrived near Casper . . . a special train loaded with men, saddle horses, three wagons and teams, ammunition and camping outfit. . . . Before daylight the party came in this direction. In the testimony given before the coroner's jury there were 52 men in the party . . . who were instructed to tell anyone who might inquire, that they were a surveying party bound for Bald Mountain. . . . Before daylight on the morning of 9th April this party of cattle barons and their hired assassins arrived near Nolan's Ranch on Powder River, known as the KC Ranch, which ranch they surrounded. There were in said ranch Nathan D. Champion, Nicholas Ray, Ben Johnson a trapper and another whose name has not yet been ascertained.

"Shortly before daylight, Johnson stepped out of the door and was captured, another man followed and same fate. Nick Ray stepped into the doorway and was shot in the head. Nathan Champion then fought off the crowd until nearly 4 P.M. About 3 P.M. O. H. Flagg, who was mounted, with his stepson Alonzo Taylor who was driving a light 2-horse wagon, came down the road. . . . On approaching the KC Ranch . . . his son was shot at. Taylor did not obey the summons to halt, but put his horses on the run to escape. Flagg, who was then shot at . . . hurried to the wagon, got his rifle and holding seven men at bay, gave Taylor time to cut loose one horse, mount and both hurried away . . . constantly shot at, but escaped. . . . The cattle barons killed Flagg's other horse, took the wagon, loaded it with pitch pine, set it afire and ran it against the house in which Champion was still defending his life. They succeeded in setting the building on fire, and Champion when he could no longer endure the smoke, ran from the burning building, and was soon riddled with bullets. His body lay about 200 yards from the house when found by the coroner."

The news spread rapidly, carried by riders spurring their horses urgently from one small homesteader's place to another; and from everywhere the citizens responded to repel the invaders. "Sheriff Angus called at once upon Captain Menardi to assemble Company C of the National Guard to assist him in repelling the invasion and arresting criminals. Cap. Menardi refused to comply . . . giving his reason an order received a few days prior, commanding him to obey no call to aid the civil authorities. The sheriff then proceeded with six men to the scene of the reported murder . . . and found matters essentially as reported.

"Sunday morning the 10th it was reported in Buffalo that the invaders were at the TA Ranch on Crazy Woman. . . . That evening 49 men rode out of town . . . and arrived at the TA about midnight. Pickets were posted around the building . . . and the party waited for daylight. The whole posse took positions in sheltered places on all sides of the ranch . . . shots were fired by the besieged cattlemen and the battle was on.

"Sheriff Angus returned to Buffalo early Monday morning, confirming the killing of Champion and Ray, and the burning of the KC Ranch. At the head of about 40 more men he proceeded to the TA and assumed command of the posse. Reinforcements continued to come in hourly . . . until about 250 men were assembled under the sheriff. . . .

"The telegraph line, which had been tampered with, was repaired Tuesday evening, and the wire was hot with dispatches. . . . Major Martin of the National Guard received orders to assume command of Company C, for the protection of life and property. . . . The Commander at Fort McKinney received orders . . . to assist the civil authorities . . . and Colonel Van Horn at the head of three troops of U. S. Cavalry left the fort at 2 A.M. Wednesday the 13th. They arrived at the TA Ranch about 6 A.M.

"Tuesday a portion of the posse had dismantled two of the captured wagons of the invaders . . . and had constructed a moveable breast-work six feet high, made of heavy logs, behind which 40 men should advance on the fortifications and take them by storm. The breast-work was set in motion at daybreak and had advanced about 200 feet when the sheriff arrived with the cavalry and ordered the posse to cease.

"Col. Van Horn, Major Fechet, Captain Parmelee and three color sergeants with Company Guidons then advanced on the fortifications, waving a flag of truce. Major Walcott, commanding the cattle barons' party, came from the fortifications, refused to surrender to Sheriff Angus, but surrendered to Col. Van Horn.

"One troop of cavalry quickly surrounded the building, the invaders were disarmed, and with the exception of one wounded man, were marched off to Fort McKinney, where they were held under guard."

The newspaper also published the names of all forty-six invaders, under a boldface heading: "THE MURDERS." Of these men there were thirteen who were residents of Johnson County; eight were cattlemen from other parts of the state; and the balance of twenty-five were, as the paper stated, "men from Texas, hired at five dollars a day to assist in restoring to the cattle barons their feudal rights, at the expense of the blood of our citizens." Interestingly enough, there were no working cowboys listed among the cattlemen invaders, although the identities of three "foremen" of cattle outfits are included.

Monday morning, the eighteenth, Major Fechet, with three troops of cavalry and one Hotchkiss cannon, left Fort McKinney, escorting the captured cattlemen to Douglas, as ordered by General Brooke, department commander. They were then taken to Cheyenne, where they were held for more than three months, and afterward to Laramie, being held under charges of murder. After more months of legal and political conniving, they were finally released in January 1893, when the prosecutors ran out of funds to cover continuance of the court actions as well as the maintenance in custody of the defendants. Thus it was, so far as the law was concerned, the end of the Johnson County War. But it meant a great deal more than that. It literally was the end of an era.

In his introduction to the 1955 facsimile of the Buffalo *Bulletin*'s report, Herbert O. Brayer, a highly regarded authority on the early-day cattle industry, summed up

"What an Unbranded Cow Has Cost"–FREDERIC REMINGTON–Newhouse Galleries, N.Y.

the importance of the Johnson County War: "With right undeniably on their side, the large cattle ranchers misjudged the place and the time. . . . Wyoming was in no mood for this blatant and illegal resort to force. Thus the cattlemen threw away the righteousness. . . . The result was a thoroughly indefensible armed attack aimed at taking over control of the county from the duly elected, though inept authorities."

Chapter 17

END OF AN ERA

There had been a good many other range wars that had lasted a lot longer and cost the lives of a far larger number than the Johnson County War of 1892. It is claimed that the Lincoln County War of 1876–78 in New Mexico cost the lives of between two hundred and three hundred men. Even some of the relatively small and unheralded cattlemen's assaults against the sheepmen in northern Wyoming had been responsible for considerably more deaths than were incurred during the Johnson County War. It was not difficult to hire gunmen for such duties, for there were a good many unsavory characters who had been attracted to the frontier West and who made a profession of undertaking most anything, from shooting a few sheepmen and a few hundred woolies to participating in a cattlemen's range war or staging a bank or train robbery. Some of these individuals and gangs got quite a widespread and long-lasting reputation for themselves, and most of them had hideout places in the Wyoming back country when things got a bit too hot for them in more civilized places. One such retreat was close to the town of Big Horn, one of the most sophisticated little exclusive communities of wealthy and titled English cattlemen; and this was only a few miles from the center of the Johnson County War. Another such hideout was in a large cave only a few miles from the town of Cody.

Of all the cattlemen's range wars, however, there was none that had a greater or more long lasting effect on the cattle industry or the development of any state in the West than the Johnson County episode in Wyoming. It was this, more than anything else, that ended the rule of the cattle barons, who for a generation had dominated the politics, economy, and to a large extent the rural development of a large part of the northern plains. It turned the tide in favor of the homesteader; marked the closing period of the big, free-roaming herds on the free grass of the open range; and ushered in the advancement of little ranches cuddled within the patchwork patterns of barbed-wire fences, along with milk cows, children, chickens, and pigs, as well as roads, schoolhouses, and churches. Not that this was not good. It was the coming of that big juggernaut of the white man's civilization that George Catlin had predicted a long

"The Old-time Cowboy Fiddler"–CHARLES J. BELDEN PHOTOGRAPH

time before, and it was part of the great transition in the West that helped to make the United States the great nation that it has become. And along with it all was the writing of the last chapter in the story of the old-time American cowboy.

There was deep and regrettable irony in the Johnson County War. Both sides were in the wrong, and neither won a respectable victory. The war left only a deep wound that never completely healed—between those who had much and those who had but little. The cowboys, still pawns of the once mighty, became deprived of sitting high in their saddles and enjoying the fraternity of their own rugged ways of life. The cattlemen also lost the richness of what they had once enjoyed. The cattle industry never again was what it had been; and doubts can be found as to how much was really gained by those who successfully opposed the cattlemen's invasion. Although the war was a relatively brief but bitter confrontation between a relatively small number of individuals, its effect lasted a long time and affected the lives of many thousands of people. It was not just a fight between big cattlemen and small cattlemen, although that is the way it appeared and was widely interpreted. It was a clash between two different ideologies, one struggling to survive against another endeavoring to persevere. The great irony is in the fact that the basic excuse for it all was really the cattle rustling, which was the outgrowth of an old and once legitimately accepted custom of mavericking.

The cowboys were hurt in more ways than one. The big cattle outfits began to condense their operations to conform to the new order of things, or they entirely ceased to exist. A majority of the cowboys were thrown out of the only occupation for which they were skillfully and temperamentally qualified. Some had spent the better

"The Green Hills of Wyoming"–JACK RICHARD PHOTOGRAPH

part of their mature years in becoming experts in breaking horses and training them for the duties for which they too were best qualified and used. Others had spent years in perfecting the skill of casting a noose at the end of their rope to tighten its grip on almost any extremity of the anatomy of cattle or horses. There was not much else they could do or had a desire to do. No longer would there be a grub line to ride. Nor was there any logic in holing up in a shack in a little town with some buddies, for there was no springtime return to the home ranch to look forward to. Some had to settle for whatever odd job they could find. Some just drifted away to other parts of the West, hoping to find the only sort of work they had any desire to follow. Some even got married and settled down on a little homestead of their own, where they could occasionally ride a horse slowly within sight of the same mountains and along the same streams they knew so well. But most everywhere they rode, their course was impeded by the hated barbed-wire fences, which strung out sometimes farther than a man's eyes could reach; and they bitterly resented not being able to ride on and on as they once had been accustomed to do. Some came back with nippers just to cut the strands of barbed wire. In some districts this became a popular practice; and there were times when this led to serious or even fatal trouble, pitting cowboy against cowboy. And there were also those who joined the ranks of illegal cattle rustlers. There were places where no man's cattle were safe from being stolen, and a lot of local residents were to a large degree living on stolen beef. And in cases of arrest it was the same old story of a jury's sympathy toward the innocence of an accused offender.

This does not mean that all of the large cattle ranches folded up and went out of existence, although the era of the big herds on the open range was rapidly slipping behind the curtain of things never to return. Gone were the wild freedom and dedication to the life that the cowboys had chosen to live and that had knit them into such a close fraternity. There were to be herds of cattle, of course, smaller ones scattered over the back country in Wyoming and elsewhere on the northern plains, for a long time to come; but the old-time cowboy of the open range was to be a thing of the past.

Today, many thousands of summer vacationists from urban areas travel long distances at high rates of speed on smoothly paved highways to visit Yellowstone National Park and the scenic beauties of the northern Rocky Mountains. They speed across Wyoming's Johnson County, over the Big Horn Mountains, and across the Big Horn Basin. They cross prairie lands where once millions of buffalo once were hunted by only the Indians; and later, within the memory of men still living, the old-time American cowboys handled the great herds of the powerful cattle barons. Generally without realizing it, the hurrying vacationist passes numerous unmarked sites where a pioneer family was wiped out by Indians, a big roundup camp was made, or a bitter range war was fought. Probably they attend a rodeo, where the big money winners are college graduates who travel from show to show in their own airplanes. Maybe in the town of Cody, at the eastern entrance to Yellowstone National Park, they may chance to see one or two of the old-time cowboys, who can still remember the days of the big herds on the open range. Soon these cowboys too will all be gone; but they will always remain a part of one of the most exciting episodes in our history.

"End of the Trail"–CHARLES J. BELDEN PHOTOGRAPH

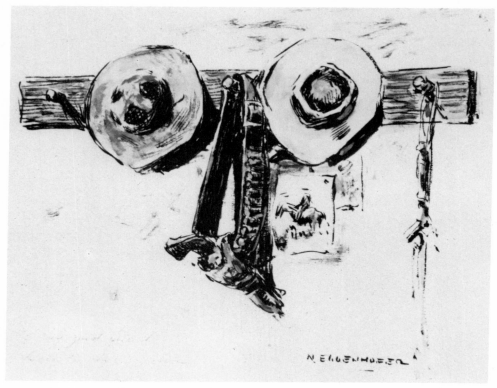

"From Bygone Days"—NICK EGGENHOFER

REFERENCES

1. Garnet M. and Herbert O. Brayer, *American Cattle Trails, 1540–1800.* New York: American Pioneer Trails Association (1952), p. 92.
2. Bernal Diaz Del Castillo, *The True History of the Conquest of New Spain.* Vol. 2, p. 92. Edited and published in Mexico in five volumes, and translated by Alfred Percival Maudslay. Printed for The Hakluyt Society, London (1908).
3. Ibid., pp. 86–87.
4. R. B. Cunningham Graham, *The Horses of the Conquest.* University of Oklahoma Press (1949), p. 110.
5. George Parker Winship, *The Coronado Expedition, 1540–1542.* Fourteenth Annual Report of the Bureau of Ethnology. Washington, D.C.: Smithsonian Institution (1896), Part 1.
6. Ibid., p. 411.
7. Charles Polzer, S. J., *A Kino Guide.* Tucson, Arizona: Southwestern Mission Research Center (1968), p. 10.
8. Hubert Howe Bancroft, *History of California.* The History Company, San Francisco (1884), Vol. 1, p. 205.
9. Ibid., Vol. III, p. 54.
10. Ibid., p. 122.
11. Ibid., p. 21
12. Ibid., p. 349.
13. George Catlin, *North American Indian Portfolio: From Drawings and Notes by the Author.* Egyptian Hall. London: Day & Hague (1844), text for Plate No. 4.
14. Elliott Coves, *History of the Expedition under the Command of Lewis and Clark: Original Manuscript Journals and Field Notebooks of the Explorers.* Francis P. Harper, New York (1893), Vol. II, p. 347.
15. *The Great Cattle Drive from California to Oregon in 1837.* Recounted in the *Diary of Philip Legat Edwards.* San Francisco: Grabhorn Press (1932).
16. Hubert Howe Bancroft, *North Mexican States and Texas.* The History Company, San Francisco (1880), p. 530.
17. Joseph G. McCoy, *Historic Sketches of the Cattle Trade of the West and Southwest.* Ramsey, Millett & Hudson, Kansas City, Mo. (1874), p. 21.
18. Ibid., p. 84.
19. Sam P. Ridings, *The Chisholm Trail.* Co-Operative Publishing Company, Guthrie, Oklahoma (1936), p. 514.
20. Robert M. Wright, *Dodge City: The Cowboy Capital.* Wichita, Kans.: privately printed (1913), p. 140.
21. Ibid., p. 10.
22. Ibid., p. 260.
23. McCoy, op. cit., pp. 237–38.
24. "Letters from Old Friends and Members of the Wyoming Stock Growers Association." Letter written by Hiram B. Kelly. Cheyenne (1923).
25. Cited in J. Orin Oliphant, *"The Great Eastward Movement of Cattle from Oregon."* Agricultural History, January 1946.
26. Ibid.
27. *Report of the Governor of Wyoming Territory to the Secretary of the Interior for 1878.* Washington, D.C. (1878), p, 40.
28. "Message of Governor Hoyt to the Legislative Assembly." Washington, D.C. (1879), p. 34.
29. John Clay, *My Life on the Range.* Privately Printed, Chicago (1924), p. 159
30. Paul Frison, *First White Woman in the Big Horn Basin.* Worland, Wyoming: privately printed by the author (1969).
31. Emerson Hough, *The Story of the Cowboy.* New York: D. Appleton & Co. (1897).
32. Clay, op. cit., pp. 253–54.
33. *The Cattle Barons Rebellion Against Law and Order: First Eyewitness Accounts of the Johnson*

County War in Wyoming 1892. Introduction by Herbert O. Brayer. Evanston, Ill.: The Branding Iron Press (1955). (Reprint as published in the Buffalo *Bulletin,* 1892.)

34. Asa Shin Mercer, *The Banditti of the Plains,* or *the Cattlemen's Invasion of Wyoming in 1892* (The Crowning Infamy of the Ages). (The present writer's copy contains a Preface signed by Asa Shin Mercer and dated "Cheyenne, Wyoming, February 20th, 1894.")

35. *The Cattle Barons Rebellion,* op. cit.

INDEX